Practical Discipleship

Jesse C. Fletcher

BROADMAN PRESS
Nashville, Tennessee

© Copyright 1980 • Broadman Press.

All rights reserved.

4255-95

ISBN: 0-8054-5595-7

Unless otherwise indicated, Scripture quotations are from the Revised Standard Version of the Bible, copyrighted 1946, 1952, © 1971, 1973.

Dewey Decimal Classification: 248

Subject headings: SPIRITUAL LIFE // DISCIPLESHIP

Library of Congress Catalog Card Number: 79-54763

Printed in the United States of America

Preface

Discipleship has almost been a code word in recent years in Christian circles. For many Christians "discipleship" is where it's happening. This interest has been both encouraging and confusing. It has been encouraging because it has called Christians to realize again that God has not simply called them to march under a banner but, rather, he has called them to a life-changing experience. More, discipleship recognizes that this life-changing experience is a process, and too many Christians have not only failed to understand this process—they have both consciously and unconsciously resisted it.

Discipleship also underscores the basic relationship a believer has with his Lord. Those that first followed Jesus Christ were called his disciples. The word meant "follower; learner; imitator." Jesus himself talked about those who would be "My disciples." Modern believers are included and need to recapture that sense of following the Lord in a daily way that will cause them to be more like him. An earlier generation was literally set on fire by asking a simple question, "What would Jesus do?" Charles Sheldon's book, *In His Steps,* was the vehicle, but the real excitement was in reidentifying with the Master himself.

In the current interest of discipleship, however, some confusion is also involved. The Great Commission's statement that believers are to "disciple the nations" puts mature believers in a special relationship to new believers which involves "teaching them to observe all that I [Jesus] have commanded you" (Matt. 28:20). Questions of implied authority and the believer's need to submit to it have emerged in this context. Unfortunately, a few excesses have also appeared that in "cultic" expressions have been tragic.

This book does not speak directly to that kind of discipleship; that is, one believer's effort to disciple another in the name of Jesus Christ. Rather, it attempts to set forth the believer's disciple relationship to the Master and, in doing so, to help him grasp its meaning in a way that will stand the tests of each day and help make sense out of whatever comes. Of course, to the degree it is successful, these chapters provide a mature Christian with printed matter with which to encourage a new Christian.

The emphasis on discipleship, however, involves a danger. The danger is that the believer will become preoccupied with his own walk and with his "spiritual innards" and fail to see the needs of his brother or to respond to the world without Christ "white to harvest."

I have chosen to run that risk because of the deep conviction that our efforts to draw closer to the Master and to be more like him will inevitably draw us out of ourselves in Christlike concern. A new closeness to Christ will make us more effective witnesses than ever we could be by stumbling along without grasping what Christ is trying to do in our lives nor responding in an effort to flow with him in the process.

It will inevitably be asked, however, why do we need any help other than the Scriptures? The answer, of course, is that we don't. Well then, why this book? The answer then follows because so many new Christians find it difficult to start using the Scriptures in their own practical discipleship. Hopefully, this volume will serve as an incentive to dig into the Word of God, the Bible.

This volume is called *Practical Discipleship* because it is the author's purpose to provide some practical assists in understanding the Christian life that will speak to everyday situations and that will, in turn, provide some keys to living everyday situations as a disciple. In addition, *practical* refers to *practice* even as *discipleship* refers to *discipline*.

I have written in all three persons in making this statement. The first person, whether singular or plural, testifies to my own identification as a disciple. The second person, used more sparingly, indicates my desire to relate to the reader in the communication process. The inevitable third person points to the generic nature of these thoughts. Hopefully, the free movement between will not impede but, rather, enhance the total effort.

The term "practical discipleship" is finally more of a prayer than a definition. It is a prayer that the concept of the Christian life sketched here might find ready application to the believer's life and provide incentive for a daily practicum, the discipline of walking daily with Christ—in every sense of the word, his disciple.

Contents

Part I The Intent of the Father (The Process)
- 1 God's Plan for Your Life — 7
- 2 The Inside Story — 15
- 3 Inside Out — 24
- 4 The Vital Connection: Body Life — 30

Part II The Image of the Son (Disciplines for Becoming)
- 5 Christ the Firstborn — 37
- 6 Christ Our Model: Humility — 43
- 7 Christ Our Model: Courage — 50
- 8 Christ Our Model: Compassion — 56
- 9 Christ Our Model: Spirituality — 63
- 10 The Imitation of Christ — 71

Part III The Instruction of the Spirit (Learning Through Problems)
- 11 The Role of Difficulties — 80
- 12 Dealing with Sin — 89
- 13 Dealing with Doubt — 98
- 14 Dealing with Fear — 106
- 15 Dealing with Loneliness — 113
- 16 Dealing with Stress — 121
- 17 Dealing with Grief — 128
- 18 Completeness — 134

Grateful Acknowledgments to

The fellowship of the First Baptist Church of Knoxville, Tennessee, in whose midst I first articulated these concepts and from whose life I experienced the supply of the Spirit.

The missionaries of the 1976-77 Spanish Language School in San José, Costa Rica, who first heard in sequence much of what follows.

Gaynell Seale, who patiently transcribed the San José tapes, and Leslie Hancock who typed and retyped my oft interrupted efforts to move from a spoken thought to a written one.

Contempo *magazine and editor Mary Ann Ward, who published earlier versions of several chapters in the final section.*

My wife, Dorothy; my son, Scott; and my daughter, Melissa; with whom I have sought and known the
    Intent of the Father,
        the
    Image of the Son,
        and the
    Instruction of the Spirit.

Jesse C. Fletcher
Hardin-Simmons University
Abilene, Texas

Part I
THE INTENT OF THE FATHER
1 God's Plan for Your Life

Does God have a plan for your life? Years ago a minister named Horace Bushnell preached a sermon on this subject and it made him famous. He was asked to preach it everywhere. It had just three basic points. Number 1: God has a plan for every man's life. Number 2: Visibly or invisibly, God girds every man for some exact thing. Number 3: The true significance and glory of any man's life is to achieve the purpose of God for him.

A whole generation of Christians responded to the convictions of this message and ordered their lives with its assurances. But that was in an earlier day.

Bushnell's three points do not seem to convince people as they once did. Perhaps it is because they were designed for a simpler age before change began to occur faster than man's ability to adjust. Now, people not only fail to comprehend a pattern for their individual lives but they are more inclined to doubt that there is a pattern for life in general.

So it is time to ask the question again. Does God have a plan for your life? The apostle Paul was convinced that he does, and in a beautiful statement of faith in Ephesians 1:5-12 he set forth that conviction.

> He destined us in love to be his sons through Jesus Christ, according to the purpose of his will, to the praise of his glorious grace which he freely bestowed upon us in the Beloved. In him we have redemption through his blood, the forgiveness of our trespasses, according to the riches of his grace which he lavished upon us. For he has made known to us in all wisdom and insight the mystery of his will, according to his purpose which he set forth in Christ as a plan for the fullness of time, to unite all things in him, things in heaven and things on earth. In him,

according to the purpose of him who accomplishes all things according to the counsel of his will, we who first hoped in Christ have been destined and appointed to live for the praise of his glory.

Paul here cites spiritual realities that dictate a God-authored plan for each Christian life. It means that every dimension of our personal existence—the events, the interactions, the circumstances that led each of us to where we are now, and, more importantly, the things that will be experienced in the years ahead—all have divine direction. The possibility cries out for further inquiry. On what kinds of spiritual realities does Paul base his conviction?

God Knows Us Individually

Paul obviously believes that God knows us and deals with us individually. Few words have ever been spoken to man which had more personal comfort in them than those of Jesus. "Are not two sparrows sold for a penny? And not one of them will fall to the ground without your Father's will. But even the hairs of your head are all numbered."

The Master declares that the Father knows each one of us. He knows us not only by our scars but by our strengths. He knows us not only by our frailties but by our possibilities. In this twentieth century when the painful awareness of our finiteness and our microscopic dimensions in relation to the universe are so sharp, this thought is overwhelmingly reassuring.

In John 10:27 Jesus said, "My sheep hear my voice, and I know them." Many of us put the emphasis on "and we know him." That's a beautiful thing. I want to know God. J. I. Packard's book, *Knowing God,* speaks to the hunger that's a part of every one of us to know not only of the reality of the Almighty but also his person. That's precisely the good news in Jesus Christ. "God was in Christ, reconciling the world to himself." Yet the joy of knowing God builds on the greater truth that God knows us. He knows us individually; he knows where we're hurting; he knows what we're hoping.

The Prudential Life Insurance Company sponsored an ad on television for some time showing some amateur bowlers in action. Their candid shots showed that there are few things more ungraceful or distinctly revealing of one's particular lack of coordination than those moments when he releases a bowling ball down an alley. The final frame pictured a fellow amply endowed in front urging his ball on down the lane with a little "belly English." The punch line of the whole funny series was that we are all unique.

But Christ's incarnation spelled out not only our uniqueness but God's awareness of that unique self. The first spiritual reality is that God knows us and deals with us individually.

God Deals with Us Purposefully

The second spiritual reality is that God deals with each one of us purposefully. Notice the fifth verse: "He destined us in love." This means we weren't chosen capriciously. The computer wasn't spitting out cards along random lines. He carefully selected us in love.

A few years ago in the city of Mombasa in East Africa I was privileged to watch some highly skilled wood-carvers at work. The artisans in that part of the country are known for their beautiful wood carvings of the animals that grace the spectacular hills and plains of that part of the world. After shopping for the finished product, a friend had taken me to a sunlit courtyard in the back where the artisans themselves, sitting around on the ground in the midst of wood shavings and examples of their own product in various stages, worked single-mindedly. Their skill was fascinating. The one I watched held the piece of wood with which he was working between his feet and chipped away at it rapidly with a hammer and chisel before taking a knife to it. Working at that speed, I marveled that the carver still had toes, but it was obvious he knew what he was doing. The finished product emerged in a surprisingly brief time.

Then he began again, and in doing so he did something that God used to teach me a special lesson. He went over to the woodpile that had been provided and chose the next block of wood with which he would work. At this point he seemed to take far more care than in the carving process itself. Could this have been what God was saying to and through Paul when he talked about us being "destined . . . in love"?

I believe that's just what he meant. I believe he chose us in love very carefully, before we ever inherited the flesh and blood of our mortal bodies. That doesn't take one thing away from our decision to follow him, but it means that on the other side of our freely-exercised decision we find that we had been wooed by the Master according to his purposes.

If God deals with us individually and works with us purposefully, then nothing that happens to us is senseless. Like the quick strokes of the wood-carver on the shapeless wood, each event has meaning.

But isn't it more difficult to accept the thought that something which happens to you is senseless or meaningless? In Christ we are precluded from feeling that we are a part of a mindless continuum. This passage says that, in Christ, God is at work with us purposefully and pointedly.

One of the greatest assurances that ever came to me in this regard came as I read the first chapter of James. In verse 2 the author declares the radical notion that Christians should count it joy when they encounter difficulty. For many, including some Christians, this is a scandalous thought. In the verses that follow, however, James shows why. He reveals that difficulties bathed in faith are converted into virtues that are vital to our maturing process.

Then, in verse 5, James voices one of the great promises of Scripture: "If any of you lacks wisdom, let him ask God . . . ." The problem is that too many people reading that verse divorce it from the previous verses. It occurred to me one day that James's invitation to ask God for wisdom includes understanding the trials or difficulties that come our way. When their purpose is not immediately obvious, let us ask. James goes on to say that we should not ask in a doubting way but in faith, our course already fixed in Christ and seeking to understand what he is about in our lives. I began doing that, and while the answer has not always come immediately (the process of the previous two verses must have its way), the answer inevitably comes. Even our asking him is a prayer of faith.

God Involves Us in His Purpose

The third spiritual reality in Paul's Ephesians' statement, pointing to a God-authored plan in our lives, is found in verse 11. Paul refers to "the purpose of him who accomplishes all things according to the counsel of his will." Among other things, it means that God involves our lives in his purpose according to his own cosmic goals. God isn't moving through life playing it by ear. He knows what he wants to do and he involves us in the process.

Paul says, "We who first hoped in Christ have been destined and appointed to live for the praise of his glory" (v. 12). He's speaking here to the Jewish people, affirming again their role in God's economy of things. But he's saying more. He's saying that each believer has a particular role in what God is trying to do. One of the most ennobling things in life is the truth that God involves his own as instruments in his eternal purpose. In the language of youth, it's "mind-blowing" that the Almighty God who holds all things together would not only be mindful of us and deal with us purposefully but would also use us for his own good purposes. Saint Francis of Assisi prayed, "God, make me an instrument." That's been the prayer of many believers through the years. Their testimony has been that God has graciously done just that.

But mark this notion well. It needs to be put in the context of a greater truth. Hopefully, before this chapter is out, that truth will be clear.

Facing the Problems

Despite Paul's conviction that there is a God-authored plan for every life, the problems for the rational mind are staggering. If you've not even thought of the problems, the following may seem like a disservice. But I believe your foundation will be stronger once the problems are faced.

First, how can we be free if there is a plan operative from above for our lives? It would seem, if such a plan exists, we are in some kind of a fixed orbit. Isn't it like puppetry? No matter what we do, good or bad, someone is pulling the strings. It all operates mechanically. And we can go around assuming that we're not really responsible for anything: "Allah wills it." "Que será, será." More oppressive is a related possibility that there is a plan for our lives, but day by day we walk a tightrope of the possibility of blowing it, of smashing it, of spilling it, of messing it up, of falling aside from it, without any kind of recourse. Jesus said he called us to be free, and free indeed. Yet how can we be free if there is a fixed plan?

Secondly, how can we be under some kind of purposeful guidance from God knowing how other people's decisions impinge on us? Example: I am minus a friend God had brought into my life a few years back. Somebody made a decision to go around a curve at a high speed on the wrong side of the road, and my friend's life was wiped out an instant later because of that decision. How can God have a plan that is operative in our lives when stupid moves on the part of other people can radically alter for us, and those around us, any kind of personal direction?

I once talked with a young student who was devastated by his failure to be admitted to medical school. He had worked hard for it. He had made good grades. But when it got right down to it, he was turned down. He said, "I could have handled that. But I realized that one young man was admitted who did not have the grades that I had. I realized the difference was pull, influence." And he added bitterly, "That thought devastates me." How can God have a plan for our lives when other people's actions are so influential on us and can even rob us of the right to choose?

Thirdly, how can God have a plan and deal purposefully with our lives when we consider the ecology of events? Ecology is a relatively new word. It refers to the concept that everything is interrelated and that all things are uniquely dependent on all other things so that there's really a kind of a whole fabric to life. Ecology jumped into our awareness when Rachel Carson published her famous book, *Silent Spring*. In it she traced the impact of insecticides on our environment. We have a little pest problem and we deal with it with an insecticide. That insecticide sets up an imbalance in nature that begins to ripple throughout our environment. She traced the effect of such an effort and showed how it makes a full circle. We've begun to realize since that time, with the oil crisis, with economic realities, and with our involvement in a world community, that all events inevitably relate to each other and that there are variables and unpredictable dimensions that are always at work. People in other nations may be making key decisions right now that will influence our future more than we think possible. I know some people who go through life scared to death of that possibility.

The Key to Understanding: God's Sovereignty

How can God work in the midst of such impacting variables? Let me ask you a question: Can God match man? If we think about it, such problems as we've posed may simply be imposing our own limitations upon God. We may be seeing God as an extension of who we are rather than ourselves as his creation.

It may be that, when we find ourselves crushed by such problems, our concept of God is too small. If God is sovereign, he is sovereign over all events. You may say, "Do you mean he was sovereign over that tragedy of the loss of your friend?" Yes. God was sovereign in the sense that he doesn't allow evil to negate his ultimate purposes. Like the potter, he can mold even the flaw into the vessel until his purposes are realized.

This possibility can be illustrated with computers and cybernetics.

Men have developed computers—analog computers, for instance, which are used in the manufacturing process of many of the things that you and I take for granted. These computers are set up in such a way that they can respond to changes of temperature, variations in raw materials, and hundreds of other variables. The computer constantly triggers responses to those variations. Now, who created that? Man did. God created man!

Or consider a programmed learning experience. You start a programmed learning lesson, and it gives you a question with three or four possible answers. If you take a wrong answer, it doesn't tell you, "You're wrong. Shame on you." It refers you to another page. You go to that page, read that material, and answer a question. You might move through two or three stages until you come back again to the original point and face the question again. Only this time you know the answer. The whole lesson is designed to deal with the alternatives that are before you in such a way that you always end up where you're supposed to be. Man designed that. God designed man!

How much more can the God of the universe, in whose light we are but a pale shadow, work in our midst to respond to all of the variables, all of the unpredictables, all of the rebellions, all of the changes, all of the impingements, the ecology of all events, to realize his purposes? He not only can, but the fact that he does is part of the gospel. The purposes of God in our lives issue from his sovereignty.

If you begin to believe in God's purpose in your own life, you will soon be pondering Romans 8:28-29: "And we know that all things work together for good to them that love God, to them who are the called according to his purpose" (KJV). God is saying to us, "Look, you are free. You can do this, or you can do that. Yes, you are in the midst of community, and other people's actions can affect you this way, that way, or the other. Yes, you are a part of a whole event that we call history, and it all interrelates. But if your life is in my hands, I will work, weave, and mold all things according to my purpose in your life."

Now, what is that purpose? Read verse 29. "For whom he did foreknow, he also did predestinate to be conformed to the image of his Son." What is God's purpose for your life? His purpose for each believer is that he be conformed to the image of his Son. (Some feel such a concept threatens individuality. This question is dealt with at length in chapter 5.) This means he wants you to become the person that he destined you to be. You may feel like a derelict, cast off to the side by your own rebellion, but by committing your life to him and receiving him by faith into your life, you allow him direction in your life, the power to make of you the kind of person you were born to become. This reality means that every day has significance. It means that every tough blow, by permission or direction, will be taken into the loving hand of God as he shapes us into the kind of people he wants us to be. Every trial and challenge, far from being something we need to bemoan, will include the tutorial hand of a God who cares. Every blessing may be the sweetening, the assurance, the love song that our hearts yearn for. But in all of it, he's working out his plan and purpose for our lives.

His plan is to make us into what we ought to become through our pilgrimage with Jesus Christ. Salvation begins it, but that's not all. Picture a person lying on a sickbed, maybe unable to move. If this grand notion is true, God is at work in this life still molding and making it. The thought that such a person is useless is ruled out by this truth. God is still at work. "Be patient," a young Christian once pled, "God is not through with me yet."

He will involve you as his instrument in particular situations. What a blessed thing that is. A friend of mine, in giving a simple testimony, once made the difference between life and death for a person who was so discouraged that he was ready to take the life that God had given him. But because of my friend's testimony, this man took heart, turned to God, received a sense of purpose, and has already blessed literally hundreds of others in the ministry that became his. The potential each of us has on others is not always a threat. It can be part of God's gracious plan.

I left the Foreign Mission Board to become a pastor some years ago. People in several states and four foreign countries were soon involved in other moves triggered by that decision. Children were moved thousands of miles and had to start their lives in new places because of that decision. Yet I can see God's purposes for many of us still being realized through that decision. We are all intricately involved in other's lives.

The witness of Scripture is that we can be sure that there is a God who is caring and ordering and making all of these things work together for the purposes of conforming each of us to the image of his Son—that Christ might be the firstborn of many.

2 The Inside Story

By what dynamics will God accomplish his grand design in the lives of those who accept his reconciling work in Christ? It is not overly dramatic to say that it is an "inside story" reserved for the understanding of those who experience new life in Christ as a result of their gamble of faith. But it is an "inside story" also in terms of the biblical language.

Two aspects of experiencing Christ emerge from the pages of the New Testament. One is the phenomenon of being "in Christ." Another is described as having Christ "in you" (John 15:4). Are there two ways of speaking of the same thing or are they two different dimensions—each uniquely significant in that experience?

To dramatize the first aspect, God has given us baptism. Baptism beautifully depicts our being "in Christ." The second aspect is pictured in a surprisingly full sense in the "Lord's Supper" or "Communion"—"Christ in us."

I had the joy of having in a former congregation a large group of deaf members. One of my associates had prime responsibility for ministry to the deaf. I worked hard at trying to learn to communicate but made only slight progress. One of the things that I did learn, because I did it often, thanks to his ministry, was how to sign our baptismal ceremony. We would both be in the pool at the same time when we had converts that we were baptizing from the deaf group. He would sign to the deaf constituency when I was baptizing, and I would sign to them when he was baptizing. The signing of "buried with Christ in baptism" and "risen to walk again in newness of life" is one of the most graphic phrases I know. The concept of "risen" illustrates. Two fingers are placed perpendicular to the palm of the other hand, picturing a person standing. When I first saw the sign, I said, "That's a great way to picture our new life." In the first place, you land on your feet. That's where the Lord

15

wants us to land. But some weeks after I learned this, I saw the deaf group singing. You say, "How do the deaf sing?" I guess I just tend to think of it that way. They were signing "Stand Up, Stand Up for Jesus," and it was this same term for "risen" that they were using. I thought, We need to get hold of that. Standing up for Jesus is the resurrection kind of life. This is the way we're supposed to live every day—a resurrection kind of experience. This is the initial meaning of being "in Christ."

There are biblical references to baptism as washing and cleansing, but the primary meaning of baptism is death, burial, and resurrection with Christ as Paul points out in Romans 6:3-5. Our baptism is a picture of our identification with Jesus Christ in his death, his burial, and his resurrection. It is important to realize what that identification means because we cannot begin to understand the process of being conformed to his image until we begin to learn what it means to be identified with Jesus Christ. When we trust him by faith as Lord and Savior, when we turn from the old life and embrace the new life in Jesus Christ, we are identified with Christ. We are "in Christ."

What does it mean to be identified with Christ? For one thing, it means we are identified with him on the cross. The death he died for us we are dying in him. Now, this is absolutely imperative because it is sin that has estranged us from God. The wages of sin is death. We must die to sin or die in sin. It's inevitable. We have to. And the only way we're going to die to sin, rather than in sin, is through identification with Jesus Christ on that cross where he died to sin for us.

Sometimes we look at the death that comes with sin as a kind of a zapping that God does on people who are bad. That's not it at all. Sin has death built into it. It's the nature of sin. It's the nature of the resulting corruption that brings death.

A concept of flight can illustrate. Essentially, what makes an airplane fly is the pressure differential created as air passes across the wings. Because of the configuration of the wing, the air passing over the top has to go faster than the air passing underneath. According to Bernoulli's principle, this creates a relative pressure difference which creates lift. So what holds a plane up is not the air under it but the relative vacuum on top of it. When a plane is passing through the air at an increasing angle of attack, this air furnishes more and more lift, up to a point. But there is a point where the angle is too steep for the air to make the journey, and it just kind of burbles.

It's at the point you have problems if you're in it because it's going to fall out from under you. When the plane falls out from under you, don't take it personally. It's not mad at you. It doesn't feel like you've abused it. There's nothing within it which says, "Shame on you. You stuck my nose so high in the air, I fell out." No. It's just the nature of flight.

Now the nature of sin is death. It corrupts God's creation. It breaks the life relationship. It brings death. And there is no way that we as sinful creatures are going to escape death.

The death of sin can either be experienced in terms of physical death or it can be experienced in terms of identification with Christ's death. I believe that when I received Jesus Christ into my life, I died with him on Calvary's cross. I paid the price. You say, "Now, wait a minute. He paid the price for you." True, he did pay the price, but he made it possible for it to be paid for me by identifying with him. I was with him. We both died to my sin there. Those were my sins bringing about his death. I was identified with him. But because I was, death for me is no longer the penalty of sin. It is now the door into the presence of God.

As a pastor, I remember the death of a lady with whom I had shared many moments in her final days and with whom I had had the joy of sharing the Christian faith and talking about heaven in a way that I'd never had a chance to do before. When she died, I was close enough to the hospital that I could be there within minutes. Her daughter met me, and in a few minutes her son-in-law came. The three of us stood outside the door praying. The doctor had not yet come, and the nurses had not yet gone in. While we were standing there, I had the most unusual feeling that I've ever had in relationship to death. I had the feeling that I was standing right at the point at which a curtain had been opened and was still moving as if somebody had just passed through. I had the distinct feeling that I was standing very close to the kingdom of God. By that, I don't mean it's located near that hospital. I mean that when the door opened to receive this Christian woman into the presence of the Lord, I was standing so close that I had the feeling of his welcoming presence.

More than identifying with Christ in his death, I have identified with him in his burial and resurrection. My old life is over. John Stout, the British theologian, has a unique way of describing this experience. He says it's as if you've been writing your life in two volumes. When you received Jesus Christ, no matter what your age, you closed volume 1. You said, "That's it." Then you opened volume 2 and began to write a new life. Now your first entry might be, "Boy, I ripped my britches today!" You're not going to be suddenly perfect. If born again, you're going to start out as a baby, right? You remember that Nicodemus had a real problem over that. He wanted to start out at his present size, and he couldn't figure how he could work that out. Of course, he was not thinking in spiritual terms. We start off as babes in Christ, but we do start a new life. The old life is buried in Christ, and the new life we lead is a resurrection kind of life. That's the reason the deaf sign of which I spoke earlier is so graphic. In the book of Ephesians, Paul talks about resurrection power. The kind of power that raised Jesus Christ from the dead is the kind of power operative in our lives in Christ.

Turn again to Romans 6 for Paul's gripping statement of this identification and its results.

> Do you not know that all of us who have been baptized into Christ Jesus were baptized into his death? We were buried therefore with him by baptism into death, so that as Christ was raised from the dead by the glory of the Father, we too might walk in newness of life. For if we have been united with him in a death like his, we shall certainly be united with him in a resurrection like his. We know that our old self was crucified with him so that the sinful body might be destroyed, and we might no longer be enslaved to sin. For he who has died is freed from sin. But if we have died with Christ, we believe that we shall also live with him. For we know that Christ being raised from the dead will never die again; death no longer has dominion over him. The death he died he died to sin, once for all, but the life he lives he lives to God. So you also must consider yourself dead to sin and alive to God in Christ Jesus (vv. 3-11).

But we still have the remaining reality of the old nature with which we have to grapple. No matter that we buried it in Christ; no matter that it died on the cross; it keeps appearing and stinking with its grave clothes clinging to it, with its tendencies and its temptations for us to live as if nothing had changed, as if nothing had happened.

Millions of Americans saw the television series *Roots*. It caused quite a stir. *Roots* is a book by an American black from Tennessee who hungered to follow his roots back to Africa. Because he had been related to an unusual family, a warrior from West Africa who had vowed to tell his story and keep it alive through oral tradition, he was able to do it. In a televised version, the book generated a tremendous surge of dignity on the part of the blacks as well as some anger toward whites. It also surfaced shame on the part of whites and a desire in some way to relate differently to blacks. For me, it was a moving personal experience for which I thank God.

There was one particular line in the series that, by itself, made the whole experience worthwhile. Right after the War Between the States, most blacks continued to live on the plantations where they had been all of their lives. Some whites, taking advantage of this opportunity, began to effect terroristic measures to keep them in their place which, in the portion depicted, seemed as effective as the old slavery. In the dramatization, one of the blacks, trying to talk a brother into standing up against this, said, "Listen, either we start living like free men, or freedom doesn't mean anything." In a very real sense, chapters 6, 7, and 8 of Romans are saying to us as Christians, "Either you live like resurrected men and women, or resurrection doesn't mean anything."

We still have the ability to live as if nothing has happened. I think it was John Stott who came up with the statement that the new birth doesn't make it impossible to sin, but it does make it incongruous to sin.

But God has not called us to act out a charade nor to deny reality. Christ died that we might die to sin for eternity, but he also wanted us to experience the victory in this life. How can we do that? The answer is, "If any man will come after me, let him deny himself and take up his cross daily and follow me." We have to learn to die daily. We must daily affirm ourselves in Christ in his death, burial, and resurrection.

Christ in Us

But there is a second and kindred reality. Baptism and our identification with Jesus Christ is something we do one time. Why? Christ died once and for all. We identify with him once and for all. While some have had false starts and some points at which they weren't sure about the religious process they had gone through before, it does not detract from the fact that salvation and baptism are once and for all. Christ has died for us once and for all; we come into him and identify with him once and for all; our old life is buried once and for all; and our new life is resurrected once and for all. We are now living that new life. But we have to die daily, over and over again, to know the victory over sin. At this point, the Lord's Supper depicts a subsequent reality.

In most evangelical churches these are the two basic church ordinances. Ordinance simply means "commandment." Liturgical churches call them sacraments.

The Lord's Supper is something that Christians celebrate over and over and over again. Maybe you are a part of a once-a-year church, or a once-a-quarter church, or an every-month church, or one of those churches where it's an everyday experience. Whatever the frequency, the supper symbolizes in its repetition our continuing need to die with Jesus and to let his body, broken for us, and his blood, shed for us, be operative in the living of our days.

At this point, I want to make a distinction that has been extremely helpful to me. As mentioned earlier, the New Testament sometimes emphasizes my being in Christ, and at other times, emphasizes Christ being in me. You can say it's just two ways of looking at the same thing. You can say it means that we're so much one that it's equally true to say, "I am in Christ," or "Christ is in me." I've come to believe in my own heart and for my own walk with the Lord that the Scripture is referring to two different emphases that are equally important.

"I in Christ" constitutes my identification with Jesus Christ through faith. I am his. I belong to him. I've given my life to him. More importantly, he's received me, forgiven me, cleansed me, and made me his own. It was by grace because I've yet to do one single thing to deserve it. I am in Christ. Because I'm in Christ, I've already died to sin. That death that awaits the cessation of this brain wave or, if I am so blessed, the return of the Lord, is a door into his presence. I'm identified with him.

On the other hand, Jesus said very clearly, "I'm not going to leave you alone. I will come to you." He was referring, as far as I'm concerned, to the Pentecostal reality of the coming of the Holy Spirit to indwell our lives—Christ in me. It is the daily awareness of Christ in me that allows me to live the resurrected kind of life, to die daily to sin, to experience daily the forgiveness of sin, and to experience continually an awareness of the incongruity of sin in my life. So when I take the bread and the cup, it is not just to act out something.

It is to affirm that I need the crucified and resurrected Christ. I need the daily filling that comes with daily dedication.

As I mentioned earlier, some Christians call the Lord's Supper a sacrament. For many Christians, the elements themselves have sacramental dimensions. To others, the officiator—whether priest or pastor—has a sacramental role. In one case it's the substance; in the other it's the one who is handling the substance. I, Baptist notwithstanding, believe that there is something sacramental about the Lord's Supper also. But for me, the real presence of the Lord's Supper is not in the elements nor in the officiator, but it is a reminder that Christ is in me.

In Revelation 3:20 I came to a concept that undermined one of my sermons. That's frustrating when you lose a good sermon. But on second thought, most of the time I didn't lose a good sermon at all. I had always preached this verse evangelistically. "Behold, I stand at the door and knock. If anyone hears my voice and opens the door, I will come in to him and eat with him, and he with me" (RSV). That's a good evangelistic passage. But then I considered its context. In the previous verses, as the Spirit spoke through John to the angels of the churches, he detailed their problems—things he had against them, things that stood between them and the purposes of God. Then he said, "Behold, I stand at the door and knock. Here's the solution to your lukewarmness. Here's the answer to your tendency to entertain the Babylonian woman. Here's the remedy for your worldliness. Open the door. Let me be in you intimately."

To sup, or take a meal together (in that period), constituted the most intimate kind of relationship. In fact, the thing that made Judas' betrayal of Jesus inconceivable was that they had dipped the sop together. For the Jews, it was the most intimate kind of relationship. It indicated a commitment that no ordinary Jew would break, much less a follower of Jesus Christ. When we break bread together, something is cemented. Paul warns believers in 1 Corinthians to discern the body so that they won't take the Lord's Supper unworthily. Discerning the body refers to relationships in the body we call the church. If we don't discern the body in terms of our relationships with other believers, and especially the need to be reconciled to them, we do take the Lord's Supper unworthily, because we are taking it in relationship to our brothers and sisters in Jesus Christ.

Jesus says, "I will come in and sup with you." It means an intimate relationship. This is the source of our victory—an intimate relationship with the indwelling Christ. Whether you want to talk about it in terms of being "filled with his Spirit," or just "knowing his indwelling presence," the meaning is "Christ in you."

You say, "What am I going to do about that old man, that old fellow with the grave clothes? About the time I think I've got him whipped and can go ahead and become a saint, he shows up." Well, he's nailed to your flesh. This is Christ's final victory. When your flesh dies, he has had it. He's nailed to it. But the new life in you, the spirit which has been quickened by his indwelling Spirit and made alive in that moment, soars into his very presence freed from that old man forever. Then you will see him and be like him, for you will see him as he is.

I know this is deep. And I realize there are so many nuances to it that I may have walked right past one of your favorite emphases and not have even recognized it. I hope you'll forgive me for that. I may have played up something that you feel is a little out of proportion. I hope you'll forgive me for that also. But I hope you'll see that your identification with Jesus Christ—your life in Christ and Christ in you—is the key to the process of being conformed to his image.

In John Stott's studies in Romans, he makes this statement: "Our death to sin is through identification with Christ. Our death to self is through imitation of Christ." The concept of imitating Christ is used twofold in the New Testament, neither one directly. First, Paul says, "Imitate me as I am an imitator of Christ." In another place, he calls us to be imitators of God, but the implication is there. Now, there's no way we can touch all the facets of that. But our incarnating his presence in our lives is at the heart of the process of becoming Christlike, being conformed to his image.

When I was a pastor in Tennessee, we broadcast our 11:00 AM service over television. Almost every Sunday feedback came that represented some special blessing that God was able to work out through this medium. Once after we had celebrated the Lord's Supper on television, we received a memorable response that illustrates my point. Most who are on television are afraid to observe the Lord's Supper because it is quiet, and they think that if they aren't up there gyrating and verbalizing, the people will turn them off. I'm convinced that it's during the time of the gyrating and verbalizing that the people do most of the turning off. But following this service, a woman who was a housemother in a children's home wrote to me. Her particular home housed retarded children. It was on Sunday morning, and it was her time to stay home and cook while the other housemother took most of the children to church. One child was so retarded that they did not take him to church. He made no responses, and did only the most basic tasks. Most of the time he just huddled in a corner wherever he was left. On this Sunday this housemother's duty was to do the cooking and watch over this twelve-year-old boy.

She wrote, "As you began to celebrate the Lord's Supper, I began to feel that I desperately needed to celebrate it with you. So I got crackers and juice and put them there on the table where the little television set was. Then I went back and stirred the gravy because I didn't want it to burn. When you took the bread, I came over and got on my knees and took my cracker and prayed, thanking God for his broken body. Then I went back and stirred the gravy some more. Then when it came time to take the cup, I got on my knees and took the cup. But I couldn't get up. God's presence fell on me. I sensed his indwelling presence. The very flow of the liquid seemed to remind me of his presence in my life. I was caught up with his presence and in praise. It was the most beautiful moment of my Christian life." Then she added, "Only much later, when the television had long since switched to something else, was I able to get up. I turned around and saw this child standing there, stirring the gravy, and watching me with eyes wide with a kind of understanding that had to be God-given."

I had to call her. I just couldn't handle that letter without following up on it. I called her and said, "Tell me more." She told me about an awareness of Christ in her life that opened up for me a new meaning to the Lord's Supper. She also indicated that new efforts to reach that child were under way. Whether I'm taking the Supper daily or not, I am dying to self in Jesus Christ that he might live in me in all of his fullness. My being in him and his being in me is the dynamic by which he will accomplish his plan for my life.

3 Inside Out

God has a grand design for our lives. The dynamic dimensions of his efforts will achieve that design in our lives through an immersion into Christ himself and an indwelling by the Spirit of Christ—a process by which our own spirits, dead in sin, are resurrected to a new life—the embryo of the grand design.

But it is more than simply reckoning all this so. His goal transcends *de jure* to become *de facto*. The righteousness that is ours in the indwelling Christ is meant to begin working itself outward toward our everyday lives, actions, and thoughts. The "inside story" is designed to work itself out! In the process of becoming conformed to the image of his Son, there is supposed to come a natural fountain of righteousness out of our own lives. I don't mean that we're soon perfect. I don't mean that we quickly achieve a place where we don't stumble. A disturbing fact about the whole process is that even as we grow in Christ, we become more sharply aware of the places where we haven't grown at all.

Let me begin this way. You probably remember during the 1976 presidential election when candidate Carter granted an interview to *Playboy* magazine. Perhaps because of its vehicle, perhaps because of its substance, it quickly caught America's eye. Many people thought that Carter had completely ripped his political britches. The people who were for him were apologetic, and the people who were against him were saying, "Aha!" People identified with Christian causes were the most chagrined, but I begged to differ. I welcomed the opportunity that it presented to focus on the real nature of righteousness. That is that it's not first outward at all. It is first inward. You see, what Carter was trying to do was to suggest that righteousness has to begin within. He said it's not enough that he be faithful to his wife in deed. He believed Christ wanted him to be faithful in his heart and mind. Of course, the press had a field day.

Yet I welcomed the incident in that it allowed me to talk to my own people about the Tenth Commandment. You say, "Wait a minute. He was dealing with the Seventh Commandment." No, he was ultimately dealing with the Tenth Commandment. For those of you who need a refresher course, the Seventh is on adultery and the Tenth is on covetousness. Why would he be dealing with covetousness? Specifically, because the Tenth Commandment is the one that turns the other nine inside out. One through Nine can all be expressed outwardly, and the Jews had dramatically done just that. But that Tenth Commandment sticks you. It moves right inside where you live and think and want.

It is at the point of inward righteousness that Christ taught the burden falls. In Matthew 5 he says, "Think not that I have come to abolish the law and the prophets; I have come not to abolish them but to fulfil them. For truly, I say unto you, till heaven and earth pass away, not an iota nor a dot will pass from the law until it is all accomplished" (vv. 17-18). Then verse 20 says, "For I tell you, unless your righteousness exceeds that of the scribes and Pharisees, you will never enter the kingdom of heaven." The righteousness of the scribes and Pharisees was an outward righteousness, as he well develops in this passage. The only way to exceed the outward righteousness of the scribes and Pharisees is to lay hold of a righteousness that grows within. The covetousness commandment turns us back within, and it is here that we must start dealing with what Christ is doing and wants to do in our lives.

The last commandment, according to Francis Schaeffer, one of the most provocative Evangelical writers to be found today, is the one that God used to convict Paul. I must confess, as often as I had read Romans 7, I had never read it that way. But note verse 7. Hear Paul as he struggles with the nature of law and grace. He says, "I should not have known what it is to covet if the law had not said, 'You shall not covet.' But sin, finding opportunity in the commandment, wrought in me all kinds of covetousness." This is the only law that Paul refers to in talking about his own sense of conviction. I'm convinced it was because Paul, the Pharisee, had learned to do all the outwardly righteous things. He had learned to observe the jot and the tittle of the elaborate rituals that the religionists of his day used to express their faith. Facing this covetousness commandment, however, Paul had to look within, and what he saw devastated him. He realized that God searches the heart and knows what's there. I think the things that tend to bring me up the shortest are those things that suddenly remind me it's no use trying to con God. He knows. I can con you, maybe; but I can't con God. The burden in Christ moved from outward righteousness to inward righteousness.

The thing about this inward focus is that the unrighteousness that Paul found within, that I find within, that you find within if you open yourself at all to the searchlight of the Spirit, has a way of working itself out. That's what we've all been afraid of all along. That's the reason when we're struggling in our own strength, when we're functioning in the flesh, when we are back in a legal framework, we're spending all of our energy trying to keep within that which we are afraid is going to find its way out.

My father grew up hurrahing the whole family, as he used to say, with what he called "Utopia stories." They were named after the small rural town where he grew up. They were tall tales, but calling them "Utopia stories" and enshrining them in a family mythology made it all right. So when I had my own children, I told them all of the "Utopia stories." But when my wife first came into our family, she hardly knew how to take my father. He would tell all of this with a very serious face and swear they were true. For instance, we were eating fish one time, and she was having a hard time with the bones. She had a fork full of fish that hadn't been filleted properly, and she was picking out the bones. Dad said, "Well, they'll work their way out." She said, "What do you mean?" He said, "Down in Utopia, we used to eat fish just like that. Every now and then, you'd be down on the street, and you would see somebody pull out a bone. It's good for you." As he told her this, he would act as if he were extracting a bone from his rib cage. Well, Dorothy looked at him for a long time before she figured out that was simply another "Utopia story."

Yet many people feel that way about their inward unrighteousness. They're afraid that when they aren't looking, it's going to work its way out. You may remember some version of the old childhood joke that if you have bad thoughts you'll have a wrinkle at the base of your thumb. The children were saying that what's inside has a way of working itself out. Because of that people tend to be suspicious of outward righteousness. They know what's in their own hearts, and they assume that you're trying to con them with what you show on the outside in terms of "righteousness."

Not too long ago, charges emerged in the paper about one of the more outspoken Evangelical figures, implying that he had been guilty not only of adultery but also of homosexuality. Remembering how loudly he had clamored for public righteousness, and without giving him the benefit of the doubt which every man deserves, people said, "See. We told you so. Anybody who is that self-righteous and spends that much time condemning other people's sins is covering up a whole host of things in himself." The trouble with that, whether this was right or wrong, is that it's more often true than not. Pride, a judgmental attitude, self-righteousness—these things are often a covering for a great deal of unrighteousness within. Jesus himself spelled it out in terms of contrasting prayers between a publican and a Pharisee. The Pharisee went to a point where he could be seen and proclaimed loudly that he was so glad he wasn't like those other people who were sinners and obviously in bad straits with the Lord. But the publican came, beating his chest, contrite at his own sin, and confessing his own sin before the Lord with a painful awareness of his inward unrighteousness. It has a way of working its way out, no matter how we try to cover it. The last commandment, by turning the focus inside, tends to expose our inward unrighteousness and our inability to cover it up.

Most people hunger not only for forgiveness for the things they have done wrong—their outward unrighteousness—but also for inward cleansing. Many of us, more than anything else, want to know that God has washed us clean inside. Read 1 John 1:8-9. It says, "Don't deceive yourself. About the time you say you are without sin, you are lying." John doesn't mince any words about it, does he? Then he says, "If we confess our sins, he is faithful and just to forgive us our sins, and to cleanse us from all unrighteousness" (v. 9, KJV). Paul knew that need.

In 1 John 2 you run into the good news that Christ is our advocate. He is the one who helps us deal with our sins. "If any one does sin, we have an advocate with the Father, Jesus Christ the righteous; and he is the expiation for our sins, and not for ours only but also for the sins of the whole world. And by this we may be sure that we know him, if we keep his commandments" (vv. 1-3).

"Lord, that's where I got in trouble in the first place. That sounds like 'Catch-22.' " Did you read that little anti-war document, profane though it was, called "Catch-22"? It was the story of an airman trying to get out of the war. There was an Army Air Force regulation that you could get out if you were insane. So he proceeded to act insane. The flight surgeon brought him in, and he said, "It's obvious, Doc, that I'm insane." The doctor said, "You really do want out of this thing, don't you?" He said, "Obviously." Then the doctor said, "Well, it's my duty to inform you about Catch-22." He said, "What's that?" The doctor said, "Anybody sane enough to want out of this thing is sane enough to stay in it."

The Scripture says that we may be sure that we know him if we keep his commandments. "But, Lord, that's precisely where I began to understand my problem. I couldn't keep your commandments." How do we develop inward righteousness? At this point, Jesus introduced us to the great commandment. Turn to Matthew 22:34-39.

> When the Pharisees heard that he had silenced the Sadducees, they came together. One of them, a lawyer, asked him a question, to test him: "Teacher, which is the great commandment in the law?" And he said to him, "You shall love the Lord your God with all your heart, with all your soul, and with all your mind. This is the great and first commandment. And a second is like it, You shall love your neighbor as yourself. On these two commandments depend all of the law and the prophets."

Though Christ becomes our righteousness, we want to experience His righteousness in our lives by the power of his Spirit. This is where we must begin. This is where inward righteousness will begin to express itself.

Francis Schaeffer, in his book, *True Spirituality,* came up with two handles for dealing with the great commandment that I had been needing all my life. He said that you learn to love God by not coveting against him. You do not covet against God when you learn to be thankful with what you have and where you are—when you learn to be content. Our carping against God, our griping, our complaining, is, in fact, coveting against God. He said the great peace that comes when we begin to thank God for everything and complain about nothing and accept as a loving gift (from his hands each day) each circumstance and each situation is the result of becoming internally aligned with our Father. Instead, we rebel against God. We covet against God when we complain.

Schaeffer believes you learn to love God by thanking God. Yet many will protest, "I thought you loved God by feeling good towards God. I thought you loved God by praising God. I thought you loved

God by lifting up prayers of beauty and doing acts of goodness." You do, but you never love God quite so much as when you thank him and just trust him in every situation. In the same way, you learn to love others by refusing to envy them.

At this point, 1 Corinthians 13 says, "[Love] envieth not, . . . seeketh not her own" (vv. 4-5, KJV). Some of you are watching your fellow pilgrims make more progress than you are, right? Has it gotten in the way of your fellowship with them? If you are like many of the people that God is dealing with in the process of trying to conform them to his image, you will find yourself again and again resenting your brother or sister. They have better living accommodations. They have better support. They have better facilities, a better background, better clothes, a better car. They even have a better testimony. You resent it all. But you learn to love people when you start thanking God for them, when you resist any tendency to covet their situation, when you learn to be glad for them.

There is something perverse in our hearts which, in the initial thrust, will almost rejoice at somebody else's problem. They get sick, and you have just a moment of satisfaction because you're still well. We can only experience the kind of inward righteousness that Christ wants us to have when we can love them to the point of wanting the best for them in every situation.

My wife and I know a woman who lost her husband. She became very bitter. She became competitive with the other women she knew whose husbands were still at home. This began to work its way out in hostility and finally in a great deal of ugliness and unhappiness on her part. Fortunately, the Spirit of God reversed the process in her life. She began to realize what was happening. She began to thank God for her situation. She thanked him for the years she had had with her husband and for the memories she had. She refused to covet against her sisters and their situations or against God for her situation. Soon there came freedom to begin living again, to start doing little acts of kindness, to project acts of grace toward others. Not only did peace come into her life, but she has become a source of blessing to many people.

I think many people sense their need for inward righteousness. God's grand design begins inside where it works itself out through the power of his indwelling presence.

4 The Vital Connection: Body Life

Spiritual progress is hard to measure. A friend illustrated this difficulty for me. He said, "You know, I don't know whether I'm growing in the Lord or not. I have one friend who constantly tells me, 'A Christian wouldn't do that.' And I have another one who says, 'You couldn't be a Christian, or you wouldn't be like you are.'" He said, "With feedback like that, I'm getting discouraged."

I said, "Well, you know that might be a backhanded affirmation. They have noticed who you are. And the gaps between what you are and their ideal of what you ought to be may only testify to the reality of your pilgrimage." Growth is hard to measure whether you are getting encouragement or discouragement. It is hard to measure because it is an internal thing that works itself out in unusual and often quiet kinds of ways.

But I'm not really interested in measuring growth so much as I am in understanding what the Scripture says about how we grow. In Ephesians 4:15-16, Paul shows us the vital connection to growth. The formula spelled out here may be, in the long haul, more critical to our well-being than education, matters related to finance, our love life, or even our health. Its implications are eternal.

> But speaking the truth in love, may grow up into him in all things, which is the head, even Christ: From whom the whole body fitly joined together and compacted by that which every joint supplieth, according to the effectual working in the measure of every part, maketh increase of the body unto the edifying of itself in love (KJV).

How do we grow? Paul says the body (meaning the church or the body of believers) grows by being joined together into the head, Jesus Christ. He uses the analogy of a body. But he says it grows by being joined together. We talk a lot about joining. "I joined this."

"I joined that." Students talk about joining a club, a sorority, or a fraternity. Women speak of joining this effort or that effort. Businessmen join service clubs and fraternal organizations. Then they look at the church and say, "Well, they're talking to me about joining something else." Let's not misinterpret what Paul means. The scriptural reference to joining is the concept of joining—like my lower arm is joined to my upper arm. It means to be vitally joined in spiritual terms that compare to sinew and blood and muscle and all that goes into making my arm whole. The joining that Jesus Christ refers to when we come into body life with other believers is that kind of joining.

Marriage offers an analogy. The problem with such an analogy is that marriage is treated lightly in our day. People come together and walk along together for awhile, almost as strangers, and then part and wonder why their marriage didn't take. Marriage is coming together to make one life. I've been married for over a quarter of a century, and this woman that God has given me has become part of my life. If she doesn't feel good, I don't feel good. If she feels real good, I feel real good. It's almost as if our systems are related. I'm not trying to suggest we are unreal. Dorothy and I have about as many disagreements as anyone. We address our grievances to one another with great gusto, and we articulate our feelings with all of the facial expressions possible in such situations. I had a friend say, "You mean preachers and their wives do that, also?" Yes, we do, but we are one. That makes those little problems more of a problem because we sense a kind of a tearing or rifting anytime that happens in our lives. Now, when Paul says to be joined together in the head, he's talking about coming together in that kind of vital relationship.

When we are joined to a local fellowship, a church, it looks like we are doing the choosing, doesn't it? We choose to join a particular church, but after a time, we look around and realize that we didn't choose at all. God chose. He had something to do with leading us, of course. But more than that, he had to do with choosing the components of the body. We didn't choose each other. Had we done it, we would have left out me and several of you. We prefer people who are more like us, whatever that is. But he chose each of us to complete the rest of us. My body is not all liver. There is some heart and some stomach and some kidneys and several other things I think I need. In this believing body there are variations in gifts and point of view and understanding and temperament and the spiritual metabolism necessary to make us a complete body. So we begin to realize that he did the choosing after all.

Now, when we come together into this body, we need to realize that it is under his headship. Coming to Christ made us one with him. This is part of our problem, however. There are so many Christians that want to relate directly to him. They want to get everything straight from him. They don't want to be bothered with you or with me. But this Scripture says they are barking up the wrong tree. If you are going to relate to Christ, you are going to relate to his body. He doesn't have any attachments hanging off some other part of his head. They are all a part of his body.

I remember one of the most terrifying images I was introduced to as a child was the headless horseman of Washington Irving's famous story. I could not imagine anything more scary than a horseman riding around without a head. That sounded awful. I'm not sure it was awful because a headless horseman is dead or because it is mindless and directionless. But a church is like that when it is not joined to the head which is Jesus Christ. This may be the ultimate problem of cults. Christ must be the one who leads us and guides us. It is his sovereignty in our lives that makes us the church.

In his formula for growth, then, Paul said first you've got to be joined together. The reason is that this joining of life to life is the basis by which we are supplied from the head. You can't just go off in a corner and trust that when you need Christ, you can just look up and he'll come right down to you and meet every one of your needs. You say, "That's blasphemy!" No, it's not. It's Scripture. This verse says if you are going to be supplied, if you're going to be nurtured, if you're going to receive the nutrients of the Spirit of God himself, it will be through your relationship to the body—to other believers. Part of the estrangement of the church today is its unwillingness to admit that. When we come into a body and begin to realize that we need each other, then our very faith is strengthened by each other.

One fellow church member came to me one day, laying out a very difficult situation. I hurt for him, but God gave me a word of faith for him. I voiced it and had a strong sense that God was going to deal with that situation in a certain way. This member to whom I was joined in faith said, "Will you have faith for me?" And I had the audacity to say yes. Why? Because we supply each other. Fellow Christians have supplied me with strength and encouragement and counsel. I know how much I need them. But I worry that young Christians might not know how much they need this being joined together to be supplied. The head supplies us through each other. The priesthood of the believer is our ability to go to him directly without having to go through an intermediary, but it also means we are intermediaries and that God chooses to supply us through each other. Knitted together, we supply each other. "Who needs him? Who needs her?" We do. I do. You do.

The Scripture also says we are supplied when we are joined and working properly. Now, the King James language is a little bit more complicated than that. It says, "According to the effectual working in the measure of every part." The Revised Standard Version simply says, "when it's [each part] working properly." When is a church working properly? When are the joints truly supplying each other? Well, the word goes back to an earlier phrase in Ephesians when Paul talks about God giving gifts according to measure. He uses the same word here in reference to working properly. Now, it is as if each of us has a particular gift in our lives, and it's only as we are working together with our gifts, completing each other, that we are working properly. It's as if I took a thousand dollar bill and tore it all to pieces and gave every member of my local fellowship a little piece. We're rich. Right? We have a thousand dollars. Right? Not necessarily. Not as long as we take our piece and go walking off into the dusk. We don't have a thousand dollars until we put the pieces together. So, as we relate our lives to each other we realize that we need the least of us every bit as much as we need the most of us to be working properly.

When there is a rift, when we are separated, when we let grudges or misunderstandings or hurt feelings get in the way, then the body cannot work properly. It's as if the joints separate and there has to be a joining again. I once saw a football player limp out of the stadium. He had suffered a shoulder separation, and there had to be a healing before there could be any more playing. So it is in the life of a church. We had a friend visit with us one time. She talked about a very sad thing in the church where she was a member. There was a rift in the ministry team, and the church had chosen sides. She said there was no life there. I said, "What has happened

33

is that your supply line is broken down. You can't supply each other in the midst of such a rift."

This may be the real meaning of that Scripture that says that we are not to forsake the assembling of ourselves together (see Heb. 10:25). It doesn't have anything at all to do with high attendance goals. It doesn't have anything at all to do with man's little banana-type promotion schemes like, "Be one of the bunch." It has to do with our need to be in spiritual body-life relationships where we can be supplied, where God can meet our needs.

Now, Paul takes another step. It says that joined together and supplied by one another through the head, we grow into a holy temple. One of my problems is talking to people about the church in such a way that they don't think about it as a building on Main Street, or across from the post office, or adjacent to the campus. The church has a place it has dedicated to worship in regularly. But the church is not the place. It is the body of believers who worship there.

Psalm 11:4 says, "The Lord is in his holy temple." Have you ever heard that? Sure. All right, but then Acts 7:48 says, "The most High dwelleth not in temples made with hands" (KJV). Wait a minute. The Scripture says, "The Lord is in his holy temple." But the Scripture also says God doesn't dwell in a temple made with hands. What kind of temple does he dwell in? "Do you not know," 1 Corinthians 3:16 says, "that you are God's temple and that God's Spirit dwells in you?" The Scripture talks as much about the Spirit of God dwelling in us collectively as it does about the Spirit of God residing within us personally to give us new life. The temple is the gathered body. Jesus said, "Where two or three are gathered in my name, there am I in the midst of them" (Matt. 18:20). And by "gathered" he didn't mean collecting. He meant joined. Do you believe that? Do you believe that God is in the midst of gathered believers? Do you believe that God, sovereign of the universe, would condescend to be present while some preacher tried to speak authoritatively to a group of people listening politely? Yes, that's his promise. If we will gather together in relationship to the head, he is there.

I am convinced that when we are joined, supplied, and growing together into a holy sanctuary of God, God is doing something with us that reaches out beyond us. The ministries of any church as they try to share with people constantly amaze me. I'm talking about the good things that are done. I'm talking about outreach to some extremely unfortunate people. I'm talking about "caring" kinds of things that have to do with food and clothes and utility bills and personal concerns. I'm talking about witness in a hundred different ways that stretches around the world. But do you know what the real witness of a church is? It's not our personal testimony to the goodness of God in Jesus Christ. The real witness of a church is its collective life, the way it lives before people. People that came to talk to me, while I was a pastor, about trusting Christ as Lord and Savior constantly referred to that church as a warm, loving, caring body. Its life was drawing them. Jesus says, "And I, if I be lifted up from the earth, will draw all men unto me" (John 12:32, KJV). A church joined together, supplied together in the head, will draw people. And in it, people grow.

But the key words are not "join," "supply," "working properly," "temple," or any of those things. The key words are "in love." It's at the beginning of the prescription, and it's at the close of it. "Speaking the truth in love" is holding our confession of faith lovingly before everyone. Then it says at the very end, "We build ourselves up in love." All of us are tempted to be passive. "I just want to sit here, God, and you fix me." But the Scripture constantly calls us to react, to respond, to get involved. Here it says, "We build ourselves up in love." It's the key ingredient in our joining. "For God so *loved* the world, that he gave his only begotten Son" (John 3:16, KJV, author's italics). There's no basis for joining otherwise. You are to love one another. It's the key to our relationship. It's the key to our supply. The supply of God comes through our love to each other, our willingness to minister to each other. Maybe it's through a word of correction or admonition given lovingly. Maybe it's through encouragement or praise or gratitude given lovingly. We're supplied this way. Working properly, more than anything else, has to do with love. There is no doctrinal dimension in a church so important that it takes precedence over loving one another. Hear that. God is love. As we come together, care for one another, allow a warm and caring spirit to envelop us and accept each other, God grows us. In such a relationship God is going to grow us individually and collectively.

There is an old symbol of a fellow carrying a little boy around on his shoulders. Somebody asks him, "Isn't that kid heavy?" And he says, "No, he's not heavy. He's my brother."

How do we grow? We grow in love, joined together in the head, supplied through one another from the head, into a place where God himself can dwell. It is the vital connection in the process of being conformed to the image of his Son. And that is the intent of the Father.

Part II
THE IMAGE OF THE SON
5 Christ the Firstborn

A few years ago on television, I watched what I felt was a telling ad against smoking. It opened up with a father and a toddler son walking down a country road. The father was obviously enjoying the time with his son. Every now and then he would bend down, pick up a rock, and throw it into the creek that was running alongside the road. The little boy would watch his father carefully, and then he would bend down, pick up a rock, and throw it into the creek. The father would walk over and examine a flower. The child would stop and look at the flower, look back at his father to make sure he was doing it right, and then follow along. Everything his father did, he would copy exactly. Finally, the ad showed the father sitting down under a tree with his back to the trunk and the little boy sitting down next to him with his back to the trunk. Then he watched his father to see what he should do next. The father took a cigarette from his pocket and lit it, and the little boy reached down, picked up a small stick, and stuck it in his mouth. Then the antismoking message came over that scene, pointing out the influence the father had on his son.

I applauded the effort because it keyed into something about human nature that we don't always recognize. That is the importance of models in our lives. One of the reasons many of us are so grateful for individuals who have known Christ and represented him in such a beautiful way before us is because they constitute models for us. We need those models.

All of us, as we look back across our lives, can isolate those people who really made a difference for us. As I think back on my life, I realize that I am indebted not only to my own father but also to an older high school friend who is now a lawyer, to a preacher about half my size who became my father in the ministry, to a seminary professor, to my instrument flight instructor, to a golf pro. These people were important to me. They were models in my life.

When I really let my weight down on my life in the Lord, I had trouble finding a model. But the Scripture says that is the reason God sent his Son. You say, "Wait a minute. I thought God sent his Son to redeem man." Oh, he did that. There's so much wrapped up in the Son. We had no way of knowing what God was like until the Son came. We didn't know that he was the Father until the Son came. We didn't know what righteousness really was until the Son came. We didn't know how to love one another until the Son came. The Son came to show us the Father. But more than that, the Son came to show us ourselves.

In Romans 8:28-29, we read: "We know that in everything God works for good with those who love him, who are called according to his purpose. For those whom he foreknew he also predestinated to become conformed to the image of his Son."

It is the intent of the Father that we be conformed to the image of his Son in order that "He might be the firstborn among many brethren." Jesus Christ came not only to show us what God was like but to show us what we can be like. That's the reason for this process: "That he might be the firstborn." Too often we interpret this only in reference to our resurrection in like manner to Christ's. But it means resurrection kind of living also. This Christ who lived in our midst was to be the firstborn among a new race of people, a redeemed people, a people who were priests and kings in their own right. Christ came to show us ourselves. He is to be our model. He came to show us what we can be. In 1 Corinthians 10:33 to 11:1, Paul indicates that Christ is the ultimate model. He says:

> Whether you eat or drink, or whatever you do, do all to the glory of God. Give no offense to Jews or to Greeks or to the church of God, just as I try to please all men in everything I do, not seeking my own advantage but that of many, that they may be saved. Be imitators of me as I am of Christ.

Because Paul had a model, he dared to become a model. Christians everywhere in the world are called upon to make this passage live. Mature Christians are to give new Christians a model for Christian living. You're going to have to allow people to see Christ in you, and your model is Christ.

Several years ago I wrote a biography called *Bill Wallace of China*. Bill was a single medical missionary in China who just never seemed to find the time to marry. There was always a war or a crisis going on, and he couldn't see himself taking a woman into the situation in which he was trying to serve. There were the warlords, the Japanese War, and finally the Communist revolution. When the Korean War broke out, the Communists, who had been tolerating the work that Bill Wallace was doing in a place called Wuchow in South China, began a real hate campaign against him. In conjunction with their offensive into Korea, they set out to picture the Americans and all the Chinese who had any dealings with them as devils. But the problem in Wuchow was Bill Wallace. People loved him. He had been pouring himself out in their behalf; he had been giving himself to them for no gain or return; he had been walking with them; he had been their peer. The Chinese Communists had no choice but to arrest him. They beat him until he died of his wounds. Then they strung him up to make it look as if he had taken his own life. But the missionaries who claimed his body found the wounds that had caused his death. He was buried in an obscure grave on the side of a river. Then the Chinese who loved him risked their lives one night by going to the place where he had been buried and placing there a beautiful monument. They simply put his name and the passage: "For to me to live is Christ, and to die is gain." He had a model and, thus, he was a model.

It is interesting that in the twenty-seven books of the New Testament, twenty-three of them refer to the discipling task. What about the other four? Why are there four books about the life of Christ in the New Testament? I'm convinced it is because it's important that we continually look at Christ as he walked on this earth—every facet of his life. He is our model. We are to imitate Jesus Christ.

The concept of Christ as the model is not new. Many will remember Charles Sheldon's little book, *In His Steps*. Thousands of Christians read that book and struggled with its question, "What would Jesus do?" But it wasn't the first such book. Long before that, Augustine, in his *Confessions*, struggled to spell out Christ as model. Then, in the postreformation period, a man named Thomas á Kempis translated and popularized a book written by an obscure mystic. It was called *The Imitation of Christ*. This book helped develop a whole generation of Pietists who made a determined effort to work out a Christlike spirit in their own lives. More recently, in a little book called *Life Together*, a German martyr named Dietrich Bonhoeffer described what it's like to live like Christ with brethren in community.

Legitimate concerns arose out of these emphases. For one thing, people said, "Christ is more than a model." Yes! Yes! Yes, he's more than a model. Two verses will amply encompass how much more. One is Ephesians 1:7: "In him we have redemption through his blood, the forgiveness of our trespasses."

Christ is our redeemer. Modeling ourselves after Christ until he came again would not do anything for us until we embraced him as redeemer, until we identified with him on that cross, until we allowed his blood to be the propitiation for our sins. He is our redeemer.

In John 15:4, we pick up two other notions that are very important in understanding our relationship to Christ: "Abide in me, and I in you. As the branch cannot bear fruit by itself, unless it abides in the vine, neither can you, unless you abide in me." In the concept of the vine and branches, we are taught the importance of being rooted in him. He is our root. We will do nothing outside him. We cannot relate to each other apart from him and expect any nurture. Yet, as we learned from Ephesians, in him we can nurture each other.

John 15:4 also teaches that he is our residence ("Abide in me") and our resident ("and I in you"). Once more we are confronted with the inside story.

He is so much more than a model, but he *is a model* for us. Because he is our model, and because the Scripture comes again and again to us and tells us we are to follow him and live like him, I believe we must recover the ability to follow Jesus Christ daily as a model for our daily living. Maybe we ought to recover some of the simplicity of Charles Sheldon's book.

But is Christ a practical model? Who can live up to him? Are we not setting ourselves up to get discouraged?

My wife and I once did a program for a group of young adults on marriage. It stretched over four Sundays. It was the kind of thing we had been reluctant to do because we became engaged rather precipitantly, if the first date constitutes a precipitant engagement. Then we married quite young. Dr. W. A. Criswell of First Baptist Church of Dallas performed our ceremony. My father tells a story about that which I seriously doubt is true. He says Dr. Criswell came to the part in the ceremony that says, "With all my worldly goods I thee endow," and asked me to repeat it. As I did so, my father nudged my mother and said, "There goes his bicycle."

The first Sunday of our program was a crisis because I was up first, and I told the group about all the problems we had. Dorothy cried all Sunday afternoon. She protested that I had been too personal. So she came back the next Sunday and said, "I'm just going to deal with the principles." Then she told them things I wouldn't have dared to tell them. Nevertheless, before the thing was over, we were surfacing what we feel is the strength of our marriage.

But one of the ladies in the group really shocked us when she said, "We don't have to live up to your marriage, do we?" Well, Dorothy and I didn't feel that we had portrayed that kind of marriage. So, like Paul, we were ready to protest. We wanted to say, "Hey, look. We're struggling too. We're pilgrims also." They were looking at us as a model and were a little frustrated by it. But when you look at Jesus, is the frustration not infinitely greater? Isn't he an unrealistic model? How can anyone live like Christ?

A spiritual principle of growth needs to be reiterated here. The more we try to understand him and his purpose and direction for our lives and become like him, the more we find that we fall short. We progress a bit only to find broader horizons than we ever dreamed possible.

I've always enjoyed backpacking. When we lived near the Smoky Mountains, I often backpacked into them. I love those mountains, but they have a way of seducing you. They give you dozens of false tops. You'll be pulling up a grade thinking, Oh boy, there's the top! You get to that place with the last ounce of energy you have only to find before you a still higher stretch. You struggle up that one and find still another skyline above.

In the same way, as you begin to get hold of a notion of how Christ wants you to live and begin to live that way, you quickly find there's so much more. You haven't begun to reach the heights of who he wants you to be.

Yet the reality that he is so much more than we can be, instead of frustrating us, makes him the kind of model that we need—somebody worthy of us. You say, "Did I read that correctly? Someone worthy of us?" You only have one life. If you're going to lay it down, you want the effort to be worth it, don't you? Do you realize there are people all over this world laying down their lives for corporations, for dollars, for fleeting status, for some kind of sexual image? You want to say, It's not worth your life. What you're going to end up with is ashes in your mouth. You'll never get that feeling with

Jesus Christ. The very fact that he seems so far beyond us is the reason he is the only model for us. He's worth our lives.

I prayed with a friend of mine not too long ago. He prayed, "Lord, I'm thankful that you haven't taught Jesse all that he needs to learn." I think I looked up. But the more I thought about it, the more I liked it. I'm just touching the hem of his garment.

Christ is the only practical model for us also because only he transcends all differences. He is the man for all mankind. He is the model for male and female, young and old, rich and poor, simple and brilliant. He is our spiritual, moral, ethical model, and the more we learn about him, the more God will allow us to become like him.

Perhaps you have experienced a personal reaction to the "holier-than-thou" person—the person who seems to be acting out a little Jesus role. I certainly have. Because of this, the thought of being conformed to his image at first bothered me. There was something in me that wanted to express itself individually. The thought that God was a kind of a cosmic cookie cutter turning out similarities turned me off. Then I began to realize that the uniqueness that is Christ's is meant to release the uniqueness that God has created in each one of us. We'll never know our own potential or why God has created us until we allow Christ to release that. It's in the process of imitating him that we die to the sin-flawed self that disguises and frustrates the emergence of God's true creation in us. It's in the process of becoming like him that we become the person we were created to be. The next question is, "How?"

6 Christ Our Model: Humility

In the last chapter, I referred to 1 Corinthians 11:1 and Paul's concept of imitating Christ. The word *mimic* comes from this same word. The Scripture implies that we are to mimic Christ. It's his life we are to act out by his indwelling Holy Spirit. "I have not left you alone," he said. "I have sent you another comforter." In the Greek, that means "exactly the same kind." He is dwelling within us. Because of that, we have the ability to become what he wants us to become. You may have come to the "I give up" stage several times, as I have. Usually it's at that point that I find anew that God is still within me, waiting to enable me to be the kind of person that he has foreordained and predestined that I be. John 1:12 is a special comfort to me: "To as many as received him, to them gave he power to become the sons of God" (KJV). "To become" is a word of authority rather than a word of power. I have God's authorization and enabling to become like his Son!

At this point, I want to begin a series of narrow views of Jesus. My goal is to zero in on a specific trait that we might try to mimic and, thus, allow the Holy Spirit to begin to recreate it in us.

Not too long ago, I read an article by a woman who had recently embraced faith in Jesus Christ. In the article she confessed how far she had been from him and how deeply she had experienced the corruption of our times. She confessed fornication, homosexuality, bisexuality, drugs, the whole scene. Then, as she came to Christ and became a new person, she was devastated by the battles there were yet to be fought. Only as she looked back did she realize that God did not teach her everything all at once. He worked in one area of her life, and then he moved over and worked in another area of her life. She also realized, in some ways, it was how willing she was to have him work in some of these areas that dictated when he began to move in. Sometimes we block off areas and say, "Lord, you can have my whole house except for this one room. I have some stuff in there I'm not ready for you to work with yet."

I hope it will become self-evident as to why, but I want to begin with Christ's humility. Now, you may be let down already. Maybe you wanted to deal with something dramatic. Humility sounds so blah. Humility sounds like what somebody else is faking. Humility makes you think of that classic individual who said last year that he had one fault—pride. But this year he has overcome that fault.

Humility! The definitive passage of Christ's humility, as far as I'm concerned, is not found in the Gospels but in the second chapter of Philippians. It's a passage that I ponder again and again and again. Still I do not plumb its depths.

> So if there is any encouragement in Christ, any incentive of love, any participation in the Spirit . . .

For a long time, I was scared to death of the notion that the Spirit might be around me, much less in me, and that I could participate with him. But it's in an awareness of his indwelling presence and my own desire to flow with him that I've experienced a new freedom in these latter years of my Christian experience.

> . . . any affection and sympathy, complete my joy by being of the same mind, having the same love, being in full accord and of one mind.

Doesn't that describe the essence of true Christian fellowship? It also shows us how far off we are.

> Do nothing from selfishness or conceit, but in humility count others better than yourself. Let each of you look not only to his own interests, but also to the interests of others. Have this mind among yourselves, which you have in Christ Jesus, who, though he was in the form of God, did not count equality with God a thing to be grasped, but emptied himself, taking the form of a servant, being born in the likeness of men. And being found in human form he humbled himself and became obedient unto death, even death on a cross. Therefore God has highly exalted him and bestowed on him the name which is above every name, that at the name of Jesus every knee should bow, in heaven and on earth and under the earth, and every tongue

confess that Jesus Christ is Lord, to the glory of God the Father (vv. 3-11).

I don't know of a passage that reaches down into my soul and grabs more spontaneous "amens" than this one.

To get at Christlikeness, the spirit of humility that was in Christ is the place to begin. Let me suggest some handles, some personal disciplines.

1. The mind of Christ in us, the humility that Christ would have in us, does not cause us to put ourselves down but creates in us a natural desire to lift up others. "In humility, count others better than yourselves. Let each of you look not only to his own interests." There is a kind of false humility that goes about like a flagellant, beating itself, disparaging itself, attempting to self-inflict. That's not what God is calling us to at all. He's calling us to a healthier view of self than we've ever had.

I read an article recently that addressed this concept. It stated the basic psychological needs of every individual include belonging, competence, and worth. Everybody has to have a sense of belonging. Everybody needs a sense of competence. Everybody wants a sense of worth. What blessed my heart was the application of the Trinity to it. The Father teaches us that we belong. The Spirit says, "I am able." The Son, by the fact that God would lay his own Son on the line for us, spells out our worth. True humility is based on true worth.

There's nothing within the Christ life that calls for us to put ourselves down. It's all right, in the popular parlance of transactional analysis, to say, "I'm OK," so long as it's a prelude to say, "You're OK." We're called to lift up others. When you start putting yourself down at the same time you lift up somebody else, you're going to make that person feel very uncomfortable. But if you can reach out to your brother and lift him up out of a healthy acceptance of who you are in Christ and the confident assurance that he who has begun a work in you will surely complete it, you've got a starting place for Christlike humility.

In football, the referees are constantly frustrating me by calling penalties on my team for pushing off. The flankers on the teams that I'm pulling for go out and do just exactly what the other teams do, but the referees penalize my team for it. (It's called "spectator paranoia.") Many times in the game of life we try to get some self-worth by pushing off of somebody else.

I had a relationship years ago that still haunts me when I think about it. It was with a pastor. We were the same age, and he depended on our friendship. I guess I was awfully insecure. I'm still insecure in many ways, but in those days it was more pronounced, it seems to me. Every time I got around my friend, I would tend to talk about my achievements, talk about what I had accomplished. Sometimes I did it more subtly than other times, sometimes more blatantly than other times. He was the kind of person who tended to compare himself negatively with others anyway. The more I built myself up, the more he put himself down. I didn't see that at first, but after awhile I realized that I was pushing off on him. There have been many times when I've wanted to go back and relive that relationship. The people who say if they had their life to live over again, they'd live it exactly the same way just don't have any hindsight. I'd do that differently. I'd go back and lift up and build up my friend. I wouldn't put him down.

"Stroking" is what some people call it. Flattery, laying it on thick without reason, only repels others and causes them to be even more suspicious about themselves if they have an ego problem. We're not called to put ourselves down but rather to lift up others. There's nothing more beautiful. But if you can lay hold of a person's actual strength—actions, words, whatever—that you can recognize, compliment, and encourage, God will use you in that person's life. More importantly, you'll begin to get hold of what Christ is trying to do in your life. That is to free you up from yourself that you might give yourself to others. Christ did just that.

2. Christlike humility calls us to relax our need to constantly defend ourselves and present ourselves in a good light. You may say, "That sounds like the same thing." I want to give it a slightly different twist. In Galatians 6:2, Paul taught, "Let each of you look not only to his own interests but also to the interests of others." A lot of energy is involved in the process of self-defense and in the business of presenting ourselves to our brother in the best possible light. When we free that energy up to be used of the Spirit of God in ministry to others, we are like new people. We're like people who have had our own psychic energy doubled because the amount of energy it takes to defend ourselves or present ourselves in a good light is twice or three times the amount it takes to affirm others, to encourage

others, to minister to others. If you can free that energy, it will go at least three times farther with the same expenditure. You may say, "Where did you find that three-to-one ratio in the Scriptures?" Frankly, I didn't. I found it in my own experience. Your ratio may be even greater.

3. Christlike humility calls us to accept the opportunity to serve as more desirable than being served. Christ made himself a servant. "[He] emptied himself, taking the form of a servant." Many people in the world aspire to get to that place where they no longer have to serve but, rather, are served. Young people coming out of school can't wait until they're telling someone in place of having someone telling them. That's the natural approach. What we've been called to is just the opposite. We've been called to abandon our needs to be served so we can volunteer to serve. We're to change our value system in Christ. We are to regard the opportunity to reach out to someone in Jesus' name as the supreme blessing in life.

You say, "Isn't it important to accept what somebody else does for you?" Oh, yes. It's extremely important to be able to accept somebody else's loving act without denying them. There's nothing more frustrating than trying to compliment someone who always gives it back to you and says, "I'm sorry. I can't accept that." If it's better to give than to receive, every now and then you ought to give the other person the better opportunity. Think about that a minute. Of course, you could build a whole life-style on that and be right back in the world, couldn't you? Jesus was a servant, and we are called to be servants.

4. Christlike humility believes that God will bring about any recognition that we need. I believe this is very apropos to where most of us live. Most of us feel a deep need for recognition. To mimic Christ, we must lay this need aside, trusting God to give us all that we need. Maybe it won't be all that we think we're due, but it will be all that we need. There's a saying in the world that if you don't toot your own horn, nobody else will. In Christ, we are called to lay aside that tooting process, trusting God to give us whatever we need. After a time we realize that we get more than we deserve anyway. If you attempt to do the will of God in your life, there are people who might want to make a hero out of you. But down deep you will realize there's nothing heroic about it. In the true sense of things, humility is perspective.

Now, let me suggest five disciplines toward letting this mind of humility be in you which was in Christ Jesus.

First is an overview discipline. Daily we must die to the old assertive self that Christ might be the new self in our lives. There must be a daily decision to be like Christ. One of the really discouraging things to me about the Christian life is the realization that yesterday's decision doesn't work today. They tell me that one of the reasons you should get plenty of vitamin C is that your body doesn't store it. Have you ever heard that? It will slough off what it doesn't need. The Lord seems to have created the same thing in the Christian experience. I can die to self yesterday, but that doesn't take care of today. "Take up your cross daily" is the admonition. Those days that go best for me are when I open my eyes, swing my feet out of the bed, slap the alarm, and concentrate my first thoughts on God—my need to commit myself to him, to ask him to walk with me, to let me walk for him, and to let me be aware of his indwelling presence. There are days I don't wake up with that thought. I can inevitably recognize that day by the string of failures that ensue. So the first discipline is the discipline of dying to self and taking up our cross—his calling to us—and following him.

Secondly, we must discipline ourselves to discern situations. We must come to the place where we can see other people not in terms of the traffic flow; that is, who gets in our way and who's going to run into us if they don't move or we don't move, not in terms of who can answer our questions or who can give us what we need or who is demanding something from us that we'll have to present, but in terms of what Christ is doing in our midst—what people need, how they're feeling, where they're hurting, what we can do, how we can help, what we can say. After awhile, we'll be alive to what's going on around us. We'll be sensitized by God's Holy Spirit to the drama in even the smallest group and to the option for a ministry in a spirit of humility in even the most casual situation.

The Lord has also taught me that if there is no one else around or anything else to be alive to, then that's the opportunity to minister to God. Did you know that he's given the saints the privilege to minister to him? He says that our praises are a blessing to him. He says that they are a sweet savor in his nostrils. We can minister to God.

Discern the situation. See others' needs—who's reaching out, who's being stepped on, who's being overlooked—and setting aside your own needs, minister to theirs.

Thirdly, let God have control. Affirm that it is the mind of Christ that you are trying to let be supreme in your own life. A very important concept in the New Testament is that of triune man—body, mind, and spirit. This concept, often maligned, can open up new understanding of what God is trying to do in our lives. From our spirit, which has been made alive by his Spirit, we are trying to introduce the mind of Christ into our minds or souls. (Additional thoughts on this subject are contained in the latter part of chapter 9.) In our rebellious state, our mind has been responsive to the flesh. Now we want his Spirit to have control. Seek to give him control daily.

Fourthly, seek out and do servant roles. Find a way to do the menial. Find a way to do that which you think is beneath you. After awhile you'll get over that problem of having anything beneath you. As long as something is beneath you, you're standing on ground the Lord doesn't want you to occupy. Some Roman Catholic orders embrace a discipline that makes many Protestants look undedicated. They are willing to do the most menial things in Jesus' name. We have put them down right and left as flagellants, while going through every day suggesting that too many things are beneath us. Seek out and do servant kinds of roles.

Fifthly, praise God for those things that humble you. That means the things that embarrass you. That includes the people that seem not to appreciate you. That includes the mistakes you make. Instead of trying to cover them up, instead of trying to deny them, instead of trying to run away from the scene of the crime as quickly as possible in hopes that nobody can identify you, confess your mistakes. Thank God for those things that will humble you and conform you to the image of his Son, "who thought it was not a thing to be grasped to be equal with God but emptied himself, taking the form of a servant."

Are you letting your frustrations drive you to your knees in new dependence? Let everything that drives you to your knees in dependence on him be the basis for praise. It will then become a foundation for Christlike humility.

Humility can be false. But such is inevitably self-revealing. True humility—built on the giving, loving, servant mind of Christ—is never false to its embracer or those it embraces.

This is the place to begin. Only a little reflection may convince you that God has been at work in this area already. In the imitation of Christ, you will flow with his loving efforts.

7 Christ Our Model: Courage

My childhood was enriched by many things. One was the brilliant colors of *The Wizard of Oz*. Do you remember Dorothy and the little dog, Toto? Then there was a rusty tin man who needed a heart and a scarecrow who needed brains. But the one who had the real predicament, from my point of view, was the cowardly lion. He desperately needed courage, and I identified with him. There wasn't a lionlike bone in my body; I had a desperate need for courage. I'll not soon forget his key line: "My life is simply unbearable without a bit of courage."

People paralyzed with fear have perished for a lack of courage. The Greeks spoke of courage as one of the four cardinal virtues, positioning it in such sterling company as wisdom, justice, and temperance. Yet when you look into the New Testament, you have trouble getting hold of courage in any traditional sense. Perhaps it is because most of us still have the mistaken notion that courage is a physical thing. That's what the Greeks meant by it. As a child, I would daydream of myself as having great courage. Growing up in Texas and being influenced by the frontier and the Alamo, my notion of courage included buckskins from head to toe and a flintlock rifle, manning one of those forts with the pointed sticks lined up all the way around. Somehow I was going to defend that, or I was going to fight the battle of the Alamo. The thing that bothered me about the Alamo was that I knew how it came out, and I wasn't sure that I wanted to be in on that. Like I said, my problem was courage.

Here, the image of the Son comes to my rescue. I believe Jesus lived out in his days, defined in his actions, and spelled out for me in his life, what it means to be courageous. Now, there are some people who will find that difficult to accept. Courage is the ability to stand and act rationally in the face of fear. That is one of the accepted definitions of courage! It's not the absence of fear. It's the ability to stand and act rationally in the face of fear. Granted, that's a worldly definition, but it will serve. Therefore, it can be argued, "Jesus couldn't have courage because he didn't know fear." I won't buy that. I won't buy it because the testimony of the Word of God implies Christ did know fear.

> Since then we have a great high priest who has passed through the heavens, Jesus, the Son of God, let us hold fast our confession. For we have not a high priest who is unable to sympathize with our weaknesses, but one who in every respect has been tempted as we are, yet without sin. Let us then with confidence draw near to the throne of grace, that we may receive mercy and find grace to help in time of need (Heb. 4:14-15).

To me, this is a courage passage. For one thing, it says Jesus Christ knew in his own experiences on earth the kinds of problems, difficulties, fears, and temptations that we know. Was Jesus ever afraid? It's difficult to find a place in the New Testament where he might have been afraid until you get to Gethsemane. Part of what he was dealing with there must have been fear—even the fear of being identified with our sins. But the Scriptures assure me that he knows exactly how I feel when I fear. I think the most meaningful words in all of the English language are, "I know how you feel." And the most tightly knit bonds that can develop between people are those developed through shared experiences which say, "He knows how I feel." Jesus knows.

But his courage is not only implicit—it is explicit. The passage speaks of a high priest who proved his courage. I don't know whether you have interpreted "who has passed through the heavens" that way or not. However, it is entirely possible that this passage refers to the realm of evil. Christ braved it for us. In Ephesians 2:2, Paul mentions "the prince of the power of the air." In Ephesians 4:8, the words "he led captivity captive" (KJV), evokes the imagery of Jesus Christ triumphantly leading into heaven the demonic hosts that, under the leadership of Satan, have tried to subvert the purposes of God. Here we have a high priest who took on Satan in his own domain, the kind of high priest who may have known fear in the process. He is the source of our courage. "Let us then with confidence draw near to the throne of grace, that we may receive mercy and find grace to help in time of need" (Heb. 4:16).

Trying to better understand courage in a period of my own life when I desperately needed it, I studied the life of Christ to see his courage in action. I saw it as moral courage in the temptations. The courage to stand up in the midst of temptation to take a shortcut is often the most difficult kind of courage to come by. I must confess, there have been times when I lacked this particular kind of courage so miserably that I'm not anxious to remember it, even to illustrate.

In another place, Jesus was taken to the brow of a hill by enemies who fully meant to throw him from its precipice. There are two interpretations of what happened then. One says he was made invisible and passed through them so that they actually said, "Where did he go?" But Luke sets up another approach. Luke says he walked through them. You can almost picture Jesus standing there on the brow of the hill, looking at these who would throw him down with the clear gaze of one who in that moment was suffused with pure courage. He simply walked through them, and no man laid a hand on him.

In a storm on the Sea of Galilee, the disciples awakened Jesus and cried out, "We're going to perish." In the face of the furious elements, he demonstrated courage.

Yet more than anywhere else, it is in his prayer in Gethsemane that I can fully understand who my Lord is and why he has in all points experienced that which I have and will experience. Facing the cross, he knew fear, and in accepting it, he knew courage.

Have you known fear? I have. Have you known the kind of gnawing fear that won't go away, that stays with you? You wake up in the night aware of it. You get into a moment during the day that would otherwise give you satisfaction and joy; then that fear appears over you like a threatening storm and robs you of that joy and steals that satisfaction. When that kind of fear comes upon you, I believe that, in the grace and mercy of Jesus Christ, you can tap the kind of courage that can help you not only to walk through your fear but to come out on the other side stronger and more nearly conformed to his image. (The problem of fear in the Christian life is addressed more fully in chapter 14.)

Is such courage a gift or is it something that we must learn? The answer in Scripture is both. In both the Old and New Testaments, such language as "Be of good courage" or "Take heart" or "He took courage" indicates that it's innate.

One of the most moving experiences I've ever had was hearing a young missionary couple relate an experience that had happened to them in Vietnam. They were appointed in the early 1960's and served in Vietnam right up until it fell to the Communists. They were some of the last to leave before the Communists took over. Having gone to seminary with them, I know something of their background. I thought, "They are a brave couple." But later, I found out how brave. A Viet Cong terrorist had burst into their home. He had grenades and a submachine gun, and captured this couple and a young single missionary. He locked the two men into the bathroom and told her that he was going to rape her. He told her to disrobe. She refused, and he threw her on the bed. She got up saying, "I'm not going to do it." He hit her with the butt of the gun, and she fell to the bed. He began to tear her clothes from her. "All of a sudden," she said later, "I felt an overwhelming fear. I was paralyzed with it, and I hated myself." Then she said, "In that moment, there suddenly came a quiet confidence. Words came into my heart and I repeated them out loud in Vietnamese, 'Don't you fear God?'" She said it was as if somebody had hit him on the head with a broadsword. He jumped up from the bed. He grabbed his weapons. His eyes were wild and his face was terror stricken. He backed away from her fearfully, and then turned and ran from their home. She said later, "I have never been a brave person, but in that moment when I had no strength that I could turn to or depend on, God gave me exactly what I needed."

In Philippians 4:12-13, Paul says, "I know how to be abased, and I know how to abound; in any and all circumstances I have learned the secret of facing plenty and hunger, abundance and want. I can do all things in him who strengthens me." On one hand, Christ enables us to lay hold of the courage innate within each one of us. He is also the source of that extra surge of courage that seems to be ours outside of anything we've ever known before.

One of the real blessings that Dorothy and I have ever had was meeting Corrie ten Boom. Have you read *The Hiding Place?* Perhaps you saw the movie—a moving witness to this woman's faith and to our Lord's faithfulness. Hers is a story of courage found in the most difficult kinds of circumstances. As far as I'm concerned, the theology of courage was summed up in one brief remembrance Corrie had of something her father had told her. She was talking to her father about her fear of dying, and her father was trying to explain to her that God would provide her with the courage she needed. She said she was afraid she wouldn't have it. Then he said, "You know how we let you go on the train to such-and-such a city?" She said, "Yes." He said, "You know, you don't have a train ticket until you're ready to go." She said, "That's right." "But when we get there," he said, "I give you the train ticket and you go." She said, "That's right." He said, "Well, God is not going to give you your ticket in advance, but when it's time to go, you'll have it." That story has strengthened many people. God will give us what we need when we need it. Some of you may be looking at things you might be facing, and you are afraid you won't have the courage to stand. The Scriptures say you will. God will provide.

A number of years ago, I was flying from Nashville to Memphis in a light, twin-engine aircraft that I used while I was with the Foreign Mission Board. I was en route to Lafayette, Louisiana, but they were reporting storms and tornadoes. I decided I didn't need to go that far that night after all, so I stayed awhile in Nashville to watch a big football game. It was a real stemwinder. When it was over and I called flight service to file my flight plan, I was shocked to find how badly the weather had deteriorated while I was sitting there wasting my time on the ball game. I decided I could get safely to Memphis, so I took off.

Soon I wished I had given up the ball game. I was in clouds and rain, and it was very turbulent. I was by myself and realized that I was flying into the kind of turbulence that meant thunderstorms. Then came the lightning which reflected my image in the Plexiglas, and I realized who was flying that airplane. It scared me to death. What am I doing here? I thought. Then I realized that it was quiet. I don't mean I couldn't hear the engines. I could hear them and the rain beating against them. But I couldn't hear the radio. I had lost my radio contact. It was a terrible feeling.

What must a person feel like when he has no place to turn and no one to talk to? That's the only time that I have come close to identifying with the absolute terror of being alone in the elements of the world. I did tune in on the Lord, however. I knew that channel was open. He calmed my racing heart, and I went about the emergency procedures I'd been taught for such moments, including dialing in the emergency number on my transponder and trying to fly the last clearance I had received. Fortunately, a navigation unit still worked and I was soon able to track in to Memphis. To make a long story short, as you've probably deduced by now, I got down all right.

Later that night, as I was flying Delta Airlines on to Lafayette, I reflected on what I had learned. I had learned that fear is almost paralyzing. I had been flying twenty years at that time. I'm one of those old, not-so-bold pilots. (There are old pilots or bold pilots, but there are no old, bold pilots.) Despite this experience, fear almost paralyzed me. Yet, Jesus Christ was real to me. I knew I was on a mission for him. I had done a stupid thing, tarrying that long and letting the weather deteriorate that badly, but I still knew he would give me the courage I needed in that moment.

Others can identify more naturally with the kind of chronic fear my wife had to fight for years. Dot, despite a beautiful pair of eyes, has been fighting blindness for years. She has lost her sight in both eyes and recovered it by the grace of God. That same grace spared her from being without sight in both eyes at the same time. However, for a time, it seemed only a matter of time until she would lose her sight permanently. Through laser treatments in one eye, she recovered her sight in that eye. Through experimental surgery, for which she was one of the guinea pigs, she recovered the sight in her other eye, one in which she had been without sight for over a year. She now has corrected vision of 20/20. It was, for us, a miracle.

When she first began losing her sight, this kind of surgery didn't even exist. Just before this happened, God gave her a refreshing experience in her life in which his Spirit became real to her. But when she began dealing with this, she felt this numbing fear coming and going in her life day in and day out. No amount of praying and searching the Scriptures and waiting on the Lord seemed to take it away. Finally, she decided that she was just going to have to learn to live with it. Then it came to her that she *had* been living with it. God had been giving her the courage that she needed all along. She had been functioning day by day and ministering to others. Many people didn't even know she had a problem, despite the fact that this fear would greet her in the morning and say good-night to her when she went to bed. Yet the courage God provided her triumphed over the fear. "I can do all things through Christ who strengtheneth me." He has not called any of us into service that we cannot render.

God's grand design to conform us to the image of his Son includes a provision for courage. It is there waiting to be called forth by his example and by his Spirit. He is the enabler.

8 Christ Our Model: Compassion

As we continue to look at Christ as our model, some may still be struggling with the concept. Christ as Lord? Yes. Christ as Savior? By all means. But Christ as model?

Turn again to your New Testament. Three passages will reinforce understanding of what we're trying to do. First of all, look at Matthew 11:29: "Take my yoke upon you and learn from me; for I am gentle and lowly in heart and you will find rest for your souls." We are to learn of him from him. Being conformed to his image need not be a hassle. We can learn to flow with his gentle understanding hand and heart.

Turn next to 1 Peter 2:21: "For to this you have been called, because Christ also suffered for you, leaving you an example, that you should follow in his steps." What could be more specific?

Turn to 1 John 2:6: "He who says he abides in him ought to walk in the same way in which he walked." Jesus is our model.

The four Gospels allow us to see many facets of Christ's glory as the incarnation of God, as the flesh model of what we are to be. The revealing of God the Father in Christ was part of the incarnation. The revealing of what we can be in Christ is the other part of it. "That he might be the first-born among many brethren" (Rom. 8:29). We are to be like him in this life, and the process of being conformed to his image is a process involving every single dimension of our experience. It's a call to a life-style.

Admittedly, the idea of conforming has some negative connotations. Every now and then we look at somebody and say, "He's conformed himself to this world." Of course, the Scripture says, "Do not be conformed to this world" (Rom. 12:2). But the concept of conforming also means taking the easiest route, doesn't it? Sometimes we conform to this world because it's the easy thing to do, because we don't want to stand up against it, because it's the line of least resistance. All right, take that insight and apply it to being conformed to his image. What we are looking for is the quickest route to Christlikeness. If we will allow ourselves to flow with Christ as our model, the process of being conformed will be much more natural. At the same time, when we realize precisely what his image is, we are going to find that it calls for some changes that we would otherwise judge as pretty tough but that, in Christ, are a part of the process.

In viewing Christ as a model, there are hundreds of facets from which to choose. Why not love? Why not justice? Why not faith? These would seem to be very obvious factors. Why humility? Why courage? Perhaps that is my need projected on you. If so, forgive me, but don't deny the possibility that they are your needs, also.

Next, I want to focus on Christ's compassion. If God can awaken your capacity in Christ for compassion, you will learn to reach out towards people that could otherwise repel you. You can minister in situations where you can make a difference, situations that would otherwise gag you. Christian compassion is both an emotional and practical response to others made possible by the indwelling Christ.

Consider Christ's experience as revealed in Matthew 14:13-16. It begins right after word came to Jesus that John the Baptist was dead.

> Now when Jesus heard this, he withdrew from there in a boat to a lonely place apart. But when the crowds heard it, they followed him on foot from the towns. As he went ashore, he saw a great throng; and he had compassion on them, and healed their sick. When it was evening, the disciples came to him and said, "This is a lonely place, and the day is now over; send the crowds away to go into the villages to buy food for themselves." Jesus said, "They need not go away; you give them something to eat."

I realize the real drama begins to take place after this, but in the first part of this passage, the place you usually rush through to get to the excitement of the miracle, we find something we need. All of us experience times when we want to draw aside, when we have had enough, when we have had more than we can stand. Only we find not aloneness but someone who needs us. The image of the Son calls for compassion. "He had compassion on them, and healed their sick." He added, "Give them something to eat."

There will be times when you, like the disciples, will want to say,

"Lord, this is that lonely place we've been looking for. Let's send these people away." But if Christ has been able to grow in you the ability to respond with compassion, with feeling, with pity for the needs of others, then I think you will find that your ministry has been empowered in a way that it never would have been otherwise.

Sometimes we treat compassion as if it's a woman's emotion. At that point, men, we are in trouble. Our Lord was a compassionate man. Until we're ready to let ourselves feel, until we're ready to weep, until we're ready to let the emotion that obviously characterized his life be a part of our lives, we will not be able to release those things that are naturally now ours in Christ.

You say, "Well, that's the trouble. It's not natural. The natural thing is to want to pull back. The natural thing is to get enough. The natural thing is to say, 'I can't handle that.' " No, that *was* the natural thing. The natural thing now is for you to feel because you have a new nature. You have a new kind of naturality. The process that God is involved in is in letting that new nature dominate your response to every situation. "Let this mind be in you."

The psalmist said that compassion was a God-trait. "God is gracious and full of compassion." Jesus revealed this God-trait of compassion again and again. He viewed the multitudes as sheep without a shepherd. He felt their hurting. He could stand out on our streets and see beyond the cars, beyond the carbon monoxide, beyond the hustle and hurry. He could see the people, anxious and hurting and needing. He could see the people walking down our streets and sense their loneliness, their isolation. He could see the children and long for what they could be. This assurance is inherent in his example. He saw the multitudes and healed them. He saw the leper. He saw the lame. He saw the hungry. He even saw the predicament of the wedding host, and to each he responded.

By the way, compassion is not always addressed to a bleeding-heart environment. Sometimes it can be called forth by almost humorous situations. Nevertheless, we feel for the individual involved and reach out in Jesus' name.

Now, if we would learn this aspect of the new nature that Christ wants us to experience as he tries to conform us to his image, we must quit protecting ourselves. If love is anything, love is vulnerable.

I think I am one of the luckiest men that has ever lived to have found the woman that has walked with me as my wife. In the first place, finding somebody that would love me like that is a miracle.

In fact, love is a miracle any way you look at it. People pass each other like ships in the night. To find somebody to whom you are willing to commit your life and then find, in turn, that somebody is willing to commit their life to you is a miracle. I thank God for it. But if there's one thing we've found in growing together, it's that love is vulnerable. As long as we're trying to protect ourselves, as long as we're trying to vindicate ourselves, as long as we're trying to come out on top of every situation, there is something lacking. Love is vulnerable. We will begin to respond with our new nature to the needs around us when we quit protecting ourselves, when we make ourselves vulnerable to those needs.

I think one of the better lessons that I have learned in this matter, and I still have a long way to go, came through the experiences of a medical missionary named Sam Cannata, who worked in Ethiopia for a time. Three times he and a Mission Aviation Fellowship pilot wiped out one or both of the landing gears on the Cessna 185 that they flew from 10,000 foot high plateaus, and they had to skid into Addis Ababa on foamed runways. That's making a habit out of the wrong kind of experience. Sam, before that, worked in Rhodesia. One time when he was examining a child in the Zambezi Valley the child coughed and some spittle lodged in Sam's eye. A virulent infection ensued. After a time the infection robbed him of his sight.

He was sent first to England and then back to the States to many major eye clinics. It was no use. The eye was gone. For a surgeon dependent on his depth perception, you can imagine how hard this was. I'll never forget hearing him speak very shortly after he learned that he would not get the sight in that eye back. He stood there, a short fellow with a tremendous amount of energy, and said, "You know, God is so good. God has given me one eye with which to see outward, and he's turned the other one so I can see inward." He explained, "In the process of going through this, God has taught me more about myself than I ever dreamed possible and more about my relationship to him. The only thing I can assure is that God has turned it in so I can see some of the things he really wants me to see. And I've still got this other one to see outward."

Later, in Ethiopia, he and his wife, Jenny, wrote home. They had been on a caravan while the plane was being repaired. It was a four-day trip on donkeys. It usually took thirty minutes by plane. Bandits began to shoot at them. They were able to get away, however, but found others that had been wounded by the same group. Sam lovingly ministered to them. He said, "Jenny and I are learning to give that which we can't keep in order to gain that which we can't lose." It's almost a cliché for Christian folk now, but the Lord knows that's the truth.

When we can learn to quit protecting ourselves and surrender ourselves up to Christlike responses to situations, we find this process of being conformed to his image will free our emotional responses and actions to help people.

I learned a lot as a pastor. I'm convinced that God took me to Knoxville, Tennessee, not so much because of what he wanted to do *through* me there as what he wanted to do *to* me there. The years there were the most accelerated growth years of my Christian experience. Sometimes I say, "Lord, I don't think I got that lesson. Can we go over that one again?" I always find out that I don't need to say that because he's already planned it. Sometimes I want to say, "Lord, I think I've got that one now. Can we move on?"

We had a couple in the church at Knoxville who felt called to minister to singles. They had eighteen in their class when I got there. A year later, they still had eighteen coming to that class. I tried to be charitable. "Well, they didn't lose any." Then I realized that (we Baptists keep records) 110 people had visited that class during that year. I thought, Something is wrong. In fact, it was. They had a closed system. New people weren't able to get into it. It's a great challenge to secure the support you need from the people who are important to you without closing out the people that God wants to bring to you. It's very easy to do the first, but it's very difficult to do the second. The ultimate blessings come when you get to the second point.

But this couple, I found, had special gifts. I received a call in the middle of the night from one of their single people. He was in a great deal of difficulty. He said, "I can't get hold of my friends." I said, "I'll try to call them for you." He was at a pay station. So I told him to give me the number and to wait for a call. I then called the couple's house. I guess they were able to hear the phone this time and answered. I explained the situation and said, "Whom shall we call?" I'm ashamed to say that it didn't occur to me to get dressed and go help the guy. But the couple said, "Don't worry about it, Pastor. We'll handle it." I found that they got up and dressed and then spent the rest of that night helping this young man. More, I found that this was not an unusual thing for them. Besides that eighteen which appeared in Sunday School on Sunday morning, there were probably 100 others that knew they could call these people even in the middle of the night and receive help. I thought, Lord, let me learn what it means to be that willing to give myself and not just my offices.

The Lord will provide what you need when you seek to move with compassion. Have you ever felt like you were going to collapse, only to experience a new burst of energy as if you'd broken through into a new reserve level? One night my wife and I came to the end of a particularly hectic day. We were exhausted. Then we received a message from one of our families that their baby had suffered a skull fracture. We drove to the hospital. There were just the two of us in the elevator. Both of us felt close to collapse. She was leaning against one wall, and I was leaning against the other. All of a sudden the thought came to me that if we would ask the Lord he would give us all the energy we needed. We did, there between the first floor and the third floor. The next couple of hours were the most beautiful and exciting of the day. We had all the energy we needed. All of the strength and words that we seemed to need in the situation came freely.

If we are going to be like Christ, we must learn to quit protecting ourselves and let the compassion that is natural to our new nature begin to bubble up to the surface of our lives. God will provide what we need to act on that compassion.

I think one of the best examples of these truths I have ever observed was in Thailand. A missionary served as a field evangelist with churches in an area south of Bangkok. One of his operations was in a church in a place called Chonburi. There, in addition to holding services, he doctored a large group of lepers in a medical clinic two afternoons a week. He and his helper, a medically-trained Thai, would meet these lepers who would come in from the surrounding countryside. Lepers there are like lepers anywhere else. They aren't all that welcome. Yet they appeared as if by magic at the appointed time. My friend thought I would really like this kind of missionary experience, and I thought I would, too. It would really preach. I could invest one afternoon and get illustrations for twenty Sundays. Well, I got in there and all of a sudden it wasn't great at all. First of all, there was the stench of rotten flesh. Then there was the appearance of people with their noses gone and cheeks gone and lips gone and fingers and toes rotting off. I found there was nothing romantic about it. There wasn't anything I wanted to preach about or even remember.

I walked over to a window to get as near to the fresh air as I could. After a moment of feeling that I had enough oxygen to function on, I turned around and looked. The missionary was literally spotlighted in the sun coming through that window. He was on his knees. An old Thai gentleman was sitting on the table in front of him. My friend was chattering away with him in the colorful, tonal Thai language, unwrapping the filthy bandages on his feet. Then he slowly lowered the remains of that foot into a bowl of cleanser and washed it. When I saw the missionary there on his knees with that man's foot in his hands, I thought, God, what have you done in his life that you haven't yet done in mine? The more I've pondered that, the more I feel that the secret lies at the point of surrendering the need to protect ourselves, and letting the Christlike ability to feel with people rise up as the Spirit means for it to and express itself in the ways that God gives us to express it.

In the Old Testament, Samuel anointed Saul as king of Israel and then told him, "Go down the road and put your hand to what you find to do." It's still a good set of marching orders for those who would be conformed to the image of God's Son.

9 Christ Our Model: Spirituality

The process of being conformed to his image involves every aspect of our existence. This means God is at work in every single event in our lives, and he's at work in those events toward a purpose. That purpose is to remake us in the image of his Son.

In considering this process, I've asked you to inculcate his humility. I've asked you to appropriate his courage. I've asked you to free yourself to experience his compassion. I don't know what you would have chosen as a fourth facet of the image of his Son, but as an additional discipline in becoming, I have chosen spirituality. You may say, "That's not realistic. He's the Son of God. That's an impossible act to follow." Yes, it is. Yet that's why he became flesh. He was to be "the firstborn among many brethren." God intends that there be many more like him.

You may object further, "But spirituality turns people off." Don't mistake spirituality for piousness, sanctimoniousness, or religiosity. Those false facades, no matter how hard we try to believe in them, leave too much to be desired. I am convinced true spirituality is attractive. I believe there is something down deep in the most rebellious person that responds to authentic spirituality—the kind that our Lord showed us, the kind he made natural. After all, he did not come to reform our lives. He came to renew them. We were dead in sin and trespasses until he died. It was a spiritual act, and the result is a spiritual result.

Second Corinthians 3:17 says, "Now the Lord is the Spirit, and where the Spirit of the Lord is, there is freedom." Some people are afraid to surrender themselves up to a spiritual nature for fear that they might lose something. The only thing they're going to lose is their slavery to their old nature.

> We all, with unveiled face, beholding the glory of the Lord, are being changed into his likeness from one degree of glory to another; for this comes from the Lord who is the Spirit [the one who is at work within us] (v. 18).

To all of you who are desperate to allow God to accelerate the process of changing you, I dedicate that which follows. God has given me an affinity with many different groups in my ministry. For instance, because of my background, he helps me to understand the worldly person who has had a Christian experience but has proceeded almost nowhere from that point. I understand that. I stayed there for a long time.

Too, he's given me a special affinity for the Christian who wants more and more to live an authentic life but doesn't know how to get started. I have a real ability to understand this person. Part of the good news is that he shows us how. "But you are not in the flesh, you are in the Spirit, if the Spirit of God really dwells in you" (Rom. 8:9). This is a fact! It states unequivocally that if you are a Christian, you are not in the flesh—you are in the spirit.

> Any one who does not have the Spirit of Christ does not belong to him. But if Christ is in you, although your bodies are dead because of sin, your spirits are alive because of righteousness (vv. 9-10).

Whose righteousness? His righteousness. It's his righteousness that has made our spirits alive, not ours. If you're waiting to be righteous enough to be born again, you're at the wrong bus stop. Salvation doesn't stop there. It's Christ's righteousness that is God's basis for our being made alive.

> If the Spirit of him who raised Jesus from the dead dwells in you, he who raised Christ Jesus from the dead will give life to your mortal bodies also through his Spirit which dwells in you (v. 11).

It is obvious from these verses and many others that we are called to live in the Spirit and in the spiritual realm. But what does it mean to live in the spiritual realm? Let me suggest three aspects immediately obvious from the example of the Son.

Living in the Kingdom of God

1. If we are going to be spiritual like Jesus was spiritual, we must also live in the kingdom of God. He came to declare the kingdom of God to us, to reveal it to us, and to help us realize that the kingdom is not of this world, yet it is here and now. It's not something we must wait for. It's something that we can experience now.

Men have perceived the reality of life's spiritual dimension since the beginning. Isolate a group of civilization-deprived people, and you will find a people who have an overwhelming sense of the nonmaterial world. But they don't know what to make out of it. With their minds darkened by their own sin, they have evolved all kinds of ways of trying to relate to this nonmaterial world and finding peace with it. But they sense it. It's only in the highly secularized world that we have largely lost our contact with the nonmaterial dimension, the spiritual dimension, of the world we live in. In Jesus Christ this is reawakened. We know that we live in a world in which there is much more than can be seen or weighed. Christians quickly find out that they are not only dealing with a world in which God is a reality and operating day in and day out in every event in their lives, but there is also spiritual warfare going on in that world.

We must learn to live in the kingdom of God, which is the rule of God in our hearts and in the world. You say, "I thought the world belonged to Satan." It does in the sense that God has allowed evil to manifest itself and to be the power of the air, but he has established the kingdom of God in the hearts of the children that he is redeeming. He has already assured the victory, and Satan has already been defeated. We can claim that day by day. We are called to live with these realities as Jesus did. Read the Gospels again. Hear him as he addresses himself to very practical things, but always in terms of their relationship to the heavenly Father. He said, "Seek ye first the kingdom of God, and his righteousness; and all these things shall be added unto you" (Matt. 6:33, KJV). Christ implies that if we want to rightly relate to him, we must learn to seek first the kingdom of God and to live within the kingdom of God.

Communing with the God of the Kingdom

2. Living spiritually as Christ lived means communing regularly with the God of that kingdom. I don't know of any single dimension of spirituality more significant than communication with the Father.

It's the way we walk with an ongoing awareness of his presence and his power in our lives. How do you go about talking to him? Some of us block our sense of his immediacy by developing such formalized or ritualized approaches to that communication that we have a very difficult time hearing him. We even have a difficult time talking to him and expressing ourselves to him. Jesus spent a great deal of time trying to teach his disciples how to pray. We need to learn those lessons ourselves.

I guess flying has taught me more about praying than almost anything else I've done. It doesn't have to do with worry about a thunderstorm or flight plan or midair collision or running out of gas. It has to do with the fact that I'm always very concerned with the state of communication in an airplane. I usually fly an airplane that has two very high frequency radios, one low frequency receiver, and what is called a transponder. Thus, I have three receivers and three senders. I'm receiving and sending all the time every place there's any receiving or sending to be done. I like to be in communication. I'd really almost rather hear an engine running rough than to be without my radios.

I can't imagine anything more lonely than a state which I've heard certain friends of mine describe—inability to communicate with the Father. They can no longer believe that he's there. Or if they believe that he's there, they're convinced that he's no longer willing to listen to them. In some cases it's because there has been such sin in their lives that they just do not believe God can forgive. In other cases, there has been a quiet rebellion going on that they've not faced up to or they're not willing to deal with. There may be many reasons. But as far as I'm concerned, that must be the most difficult condition a Christian could possibly face.

You say, "Well, I've never lost my communication with the Father. I've been talking to him regularly. It's just that I don't hear him." Have you ever had that problem? You might be the kind that would start worrying if you did hear him.

Sometime back a friend of mine, also a pilot, hadn't flown in a good while. He had a short flight to make, but he felt he had lost his proficiency for instrument flight. The weather wasn't too bad, but it was definitely instrument conditions. He asked me if I would go along with him for safety's sake. I said I'd be happy to do that.

We received our clearance and took off. At 300 or 400 feet, we were in the "soup," and I found myself tense, waiting to pounce on the controls in case I needed to. I shouldn't have worried. Everything he had ever learned came back to him quickly—with one exception: He couldn't hear his number being called. He'd been out of it so long, he had grown unused to hearing his number. Departure control called out a new heading. Andy didn't hear his number out of all the chatter. He just sat there holding the last heading.

I said, "Andy, that's us."

He replied, "Sorry, what did he say?"

I gave him the heading, and he turned to that heading. In a minute the controller called back with new instructions. There's a lot of chatter going on all the time, and you have to be listening to hear what is being directed to you. The controller cleared us to a new altitude. Andy remained pegged on the old one. Again I said, "Andy, he's talking to us." Again he apologized, "What did he say?" "He said to climb." "OK." Then he put it up there smoothly. It took him quite awhile to learn to hear the controller again.

I have felt like that as a Christian, and I have known others who could identify with the feeling. They've come to the place where they just can't hear the Lord. On the other hand, perhaps you've had the experience of being so finely tuned to him that in almost every situation all day long, you had a sense of his presence and leadership. I've had that at times. It usually happens on days when I wake up praising God, feeling close to him, desiring more than anything else in the world to walk with him, wanting to know his will in every dimension of my life. Then I can hear him.

On the other hand, I've known days in my life, and I regret to confess it, when I arose preoccupied by a thousand things. If I checked in at all, it might as well have been, "Lord, I'm still here and I'm grateful, but I'm going to be busy today." I may not have said it just that way, but it sounded that way.

We need to communicate with the Father. If we're going to live in the kingdom of God and try to live spiritual lives, we have to learn to communicate with him. It's impossible to live the spiritual life apart from prayer. If you want one place to dig in to develop a deeper spiritual sensitivity, here it is. Pray. Wait on the Father. Seek him out.

Led by the Spirit of God

3. Living a spiritual life as Jesus lived it means being led by the Spirit of the God of the kingdom. Jesus' ministry began as he was

"led up by the Spirit" (Matt. 4:1). Let me call your attention to Galatians 5:25: "If we live by the Spirit, let us also walk by the Spirit." Now read verse 16: "But I say, walk by the Spirit, and do not gratify the desires of the flesh."

My understanding of the nature of salvation and what takes place in our beings is critical to what follows. I understand myself in three ways. I understand myself as flesh. I understand myself as mind or soul, primarily represented by my conscious, rational, volitional, emotional life. Finally, I see myself as spirit because I was created in the image of God. "In the image of God created he them."

But the Scripture says my spirit is dead in trespasses and sin. Because my spirit is dead in trespasses and sin, the flesh will surely die. "The wages of sin is death." I am in the process of dying. I am locked in the corruption that has taken hold in my mind and soul that has brought about the death of my spirit, and I am dying. Then, God, in his love and mercy reaches out to me in Jesus Christ to redeem me. Christ pays the penalty of sin for me. He becomes my sin, and he dies for me. When I accept his righteousness and his death in behalf of my sin, God comes in and quickens my spirit with his Spirit. I live again, and he lives in my quickened spirit.

But we were trained to live in the flesh. Our mind has been responsive to the flesh. So when God quickens our spirit and begins a new life in us, the life that will one day stand before God in the wholeness and newness of what he's created, that new spirit must wrest control of our mind from its habitual response to the flesh nature. This is a process. "Let this mind be in you, which was also in Christ Jesus" (Phil. 2:5, KJV).

Day by day, in every event that takes place, all things work together for good for them that love God and are the called according to his purpose of being conformed to the image of his Son. I see this three-way event going on in all of this. My spirit, which has been made alive by his presence, becomes the seat of his dwelling place in my life and increasingly battles for the control of my mind and soul. The trouble is that I have a tremendous reluctance to give up my soulishness, to give up living in the habits that were responsive to the flesh life and live in the spiritual life. Theologically, the process is called "sanctification." When it's complete and we stand before him, it's called "glorification." We are in the process of being sanctified now. It's the process of being conformed to the image of his Son. The key is the Spirit in our lives. The absolute necessity to be filled with the Spirit so that the Spirit is in control of our minds is obvious.

I don't know how computer-oriented you are, but computers present an interesting set of mirrors to man. I call them an interesting set of mirrors because we've created the computer. We are its creator. Somehow, having created it, we now look at it as a mirror in trying to understand ourselves. We try to understand how God might be working with us through this model that we created out of our fallen condition. The computer is limited. It brings us face to face with the limits of our own rational being. That is the reason we are so absolutely dependent on the Word of God as the Spirit makes it alive and reaches up beyond our rational limitations to show us what truth is. In a computer, there are three basic components. There's the hardware. That's what you see out there with all of the little buttons and lights flashing. Some cynics say most of that was built by the engineers to impress the people watching. Then there is the memory system. That's where you store all the data. There are all kinds of memory systems. There are punch cards, reels of tape, magnetic discs for random selection, and now the great miniaturization revolution. Finally, there's the program. The program is called "software" in computer terminology. Now, the machine can be the finest machine in the work, and the memory bank can be the most massive and versatile in the world, but the program is what makes it happen. The program is the set of instructions that the individual has given the machine to work with what's in the data bank.

The machine is like our flesh. The memory bank, at this point, has to do with everything we've learned. One of the problems about putting the wrong kind of stuff in there is that it tends to come out in ways that you don't need it. The program is essentially your mind, your rational process. It's this process that the Spirit must get hold of in our lives. "Let this mind be in you which was in Christ Jesus" means being spiritually reprogrammed.

We must program ourselves to live in the kingdom of God with Christ sovereign in our lives, aware that everything is vibrant with his activity and that everything is significant in relationship to his purposes. If we seek first that reality in our lives, then all of the material concerns that we might have will be taken care of for us.

We must program ourselves to communicate with the Father day in and day out until it is as natural as breathing. Also, we must be sensitive to his indwelling presence, asking him to lead us and manifest his sovereignty in our lives.

To illustrate: "Brethren, if a man is overtaken in any trespass, you who are spiritual should restore him in a spirit of gentleness" (Gal. 6:1). If you know the background of the Galatians, you know that Paul is trying to work with some people who have tried to undermine him. You have to ask yourself first, "Is his tongue in his cheek?" There are points where the Spirit allowed Paul to be a little caustic. But I've decided, partly because of my own experience, that he is not being facetious. He's being serious. In the midst of the fellowship in the Galatian church, there were those people who were far enough along in this program to where they gave off an aura of authentic, honest, attractive spirituality. Such spirituality is in the image of the Son.

Paul says, "Brethren, help this man overtaken in trespasses." What should they do to him? "Restore him in a spirit of gentleness." The kind of spirituality that points a long, bony finger and accuses is not the spirituality that Paul is talking about here. It's not the kind that Jesus lived before us. He's talking about spirituality that reaches out in love with a spirit of gentleness to lead the erring brother back.

But read on: "[But] look to yourself, lest you too be tempted." If you think being spiritual is going to eliminate the temptation process, this verse should speak to you. In fact, about the time you really begin to make progress in this area, look out! Satan is not going to let you alone. But God will buy up the opportunity to strengthen you if you will let him. "There hath no temptation taken you but such as is common to man" (1 Cor. 10:13, KJV). Do you know this verse? It's one of the beautiful promises of Scripture. (This passage will be discussed further in the chapter on stress.)

Finally, turn to Galatians 5:18: "If you are led by the Spirit you are not under the law. Now the works of the flesh are plain." Remember in verse 16 Paul said, "Do not gratify the desires of the flesh." What desires does he name? Immorality, impurity, licentiousness, idolatry, sorcery, enmity, strife, jealousy, anger, selfishness, dissension, party spirit, envy, drunkenness, carousing.

If these aren't to go in the spiritual life, what will replace them? Look at verse 22: "But the fruit of the Spirit is love, joy, peace, patience, kindness, goodness, faithfulness, gentleness, self-control." When you get right down to it, that's what spirituality is all about. "If we live by the Spirit, let us also walk by the Spirit."

10 The Imitation of Christ

Are you convinced that Christ is a practical model for your life? No matter how carnal, how fleshly, how this-world oriented, how selfish, how narcissistic, how egotistical (to be redundant) you might be, no matter how hedonistic your philosophy might be, Christ can change all of that. He can reorient your life. The whole notion of the imitation of Jesus Christ follows upon that possibility. The four traits outlined by way of trying to understand how you could begin to work Christlike dimensions into your life are humility, courage, compassion, and spirituality. But they are only that—places to begin. The real task is to convince yourself that this is something you were born (again) to do.

The Principle

To make sure you understand what to do and then to make sure you understand how to do it, I am going to address both the principle and the practice of the imitation of Christ. In so many walks of life you master the practice of a skill, but you never really understand the principle of it. So anytime it goes wrong, anytime it is out of sync, you're in trouble. Any golf pro will tell you that you can develop a golf swing pretty easily, but unless you understand what makes that little ball do what it does, after awhile you are going to have some things happen to you that will not only ruin your whole day but will also completely puzzle you. This is certainly true in aviation. Many instructors say they can teach anybody to fly, but some students have a natural feel for aerodynamics. That craft can respond to them almost as if it were an extension of their own body. But all of a sudden, something is wrong and they don't understand the systems; they don't understand the dynamics involved. They are lost in a sea of air.

Now, to understand the principle of imitating Jesus Christ, consider three words that I think will help you. The three words are purpose, power, and process.

Purpose

The Scripture says it is God's purpose for your life to be like Jesus Christ. This is the essence of what he has had in mind for you since eternity. "We know that all things work together for good to them that love God, to them who are the called according to his purpose. For whom he did foreknow, he did also predestinate to be conformed to the image of his Son" (Rom. 8:28-29, KJV). This is what God is trying to do in your life. But let's be honest. There is nothing that sounds blander than a bunch of look-alike people who act alike, think alike, and react alike. In every situation they are predictably alike. That thought leaves us cold. Yet you could say, "Isn't this what you are talking about? Aren't you talking about us all becoming just like Jesus?" Yes, that's what I'm talking about, but the result is quite different from what you might imagine. The result is the realization of who we are really meant to be, and that realization frees individualities which Paul says, in 1 Corinthians 15, differ as one star differs in glory from another star, as sun from moon.

Somehow as the heavens differ, somehow as all creation is so infinitely different in its varieties and yet makes up the drama of the whole, as a symphony orchestra is made up of instruments that are completely different from each other in sound and even in structure and yet together become the harmony of the whole, so God would have us to be different and yet conformed to the unifying image of his Son.

What we're talking about when we talk about imitating Christ is setting in motion those processes that will allow us to become what he wants us to become. He has a purpose for our lives. Being a Christian is not a fire insurance kind of experience. To imply it is, is greatly to demean the tremendous adventure God set out upon when he sent his Son into history and into our lives to redeem us. It wasn't simply to provide people with an after-I-die kind of answer. It was to make new persons.

Power

The believer is not passive in this. God has granted us the power to participate. John 1:12 says, "As many as received him, to them gave he the power to become the sons of God, even to them that believe on his name" (KJV). Jesus takes up residence in our lives when we receive him as Lord and Savior. His Holy Spirit takes up a recreative presence in our lives. He begins a process there which many of us stifle and all but put out. This is what is meant by "quenching the Spirit." Were it not for the persistent love of God, we might. But we find that when we begin to cooperate, when we begin to respond to the notion of being like he wants us to be, then that power is released, and some dramatic things begin to happen to us.

Some people feel they have been all but left out in the things that God is doing in the world today. They hear about answered prayer, but it never happens to them. They listen to testimonies of minor and major miracles, but they've never seen one. They hear people talking about the power that changes their lives, allows them to perform great acts of personal discipline, makes radical changes in their whole life-style, but they can't manage it. Why? One reason is that they stay out on the edge. They never move into the center of God's will, God's purpose for their lives. But when they do begin to move into it, they are drawn into the vortex of his power. The excitement in their lives defies any other explanation.

Process

But it is a process. It doesn't happen overnight. Some of you could afford, with a lot of reason, to be discouraged about what God is doing in your life because it seems the more progress you make, the further you have to go. Let's remind ourselves again of the principle involved here. About the time you think you have gotten to the point where you can live the kind of life God wants you to live, you suddenly find yourself disappointing not only God but also yourself. A realization of the process of growth makes you more sensitive to what needs to be as well as what is. It is a process. It has to go on.

The passage that we have looked at so often, Romans 8:28-29, gives us the nature of the process: "And we know that all things work together for good." All things are interacting when we become God's children, through Christ, to work out this process in us. We say, "Oh, Lord, why did you let this happen to me?" or "Lord, I don't understand why that happened to my friend or my loved one."

Faith reaches out and says that God is making all of this a part of his purpose for us.

Let me again be personal. One of my friends said, "Jess, the trouble with your preaching and writing is that after awhile you don't have any secrets." For many years (as I have said earlier), Dorothy fought blindness. One day we had a call from New York City. It was a man asking us to make a trip up there. (They were asking Dorothy specifically. I was invited along as the escort.) They asked us to make the trip for the Lasker Award ceremonies for Mr. Julius Stein who funded the research responsible for the particular instrument used in the eye surgery that restored her sight. They felt that nothing would dramatize the effectiveness of his philanthropy more than someone who had actually benefited from it. The trip precipitated a whole new round of nostalgia for us as we talked about what we had been through those years when we thought blindness was inevitable. Dorothy has always been good to look at, but now she can look at others, too. But as we looked back, we discovered we were not only grateful for the recovery but for the process through which God did it. We know people better than ourselves, more deserving than we could ever be, who have not had this kind of blessing. Yet we are convinced that in their lives, as well as in ours, God is working out his purpose through a sovereign process to make us into what he wants us to be. We are not passive in it, as I've said before. But it is a process in which God is involved, and we can run up a dead-end street, come back, and find God still patiently waiting to redirect our paths.

The Practice: Humility

Now, that's the principle: purpose, power, and process. But the practice is the thing. How do you get there from where you are now? How do you begin to incorporate some of these things? It's well enough to write about humility and courage and compassion and spirituality, but how do you incorporate these things into your life? Would you believe I'm going to try to tell you? I may be getting way out on a limb, but I believe that too often we shy away from the practical application of our faith. I'm going to give you three suggested actions for each of those Christlike characteristics. These actions or practices might help you begin to work out the principle.

The first characteristic cited was humility. Humility is not the meek and mild figure of the Caspar Milquetoast cartoons. Rather, it has to do with the mission that God was about in Christ. Jesus said it was not a thing to be grasped to be equal with God. He said in effect, "I will step down in this mission. I will make myself as a man. I will become as a servant." That's why he washed the disciples' feet. That's the kind of humility we're talking about. Here are three practices that help develop that kind of humility.

Turn the Other Cheek

First, turn the other cheek. In Matthew 5:39, Jesus said, "When you are struck on the right cheek, turn the other cheek also." It says the right cheek. How are you hit on the right cheek? Most people are right-handed. If they were to strike you, you would be hit on the left cheek. To be struck on your right cheek, you usually are backhanded. Since time began, the backhand strike has been an insult. I believe Jesus was getting more at our response to somebody attacking our self-image, our pride, than he was to when somebody attacks us physically.

When I ask you to learn to turn the other cheek, I'm saying avoid letting your pride get so high that you are constantly defending yourself, constantly cutting with words because you feel you have been cut. My family kids me when someone tries for a parking place only to have somebody else screech in ahead. They say that means turn the other fender also.

Prefer Others

Secondly, seek to prefer others in every way. Strive for that point where you are willing to accept your worth in Jesus Christ. Given that, it's not important for you to triumph over anybody else. You are free to prefer them. This doesn't get in the way of excellence at all. John Gardner wrote one of the finest books ever written a few years ago on the quest for excellence. I believe it is a noble trait. But the ability to prefer one another is part of the quest for excellence. In Romans 12:10, Paul admonishes us saying "In honour preferring one another" (KJV). It's not just stepping back and grumbling and saying, "OK. You go ahead." But in honor prefer one another. Elicit joy from the opportunity.

Thirdly, leave your public relations to God. That's hard, isn't it? We're so concerned about our reputations. But the Scripture says, "[Christ] made himself of no reputation." He didn't feel the need to tout himself, to toot his own horn, to set himself carefully in situations where he would be noticed and applauded and appreciated. The tremendous amount of energy most of us spend in our own public relations could be so beautifully employed in other ways. I don't know of a single group of people, professional or otherwise, more troubled by this particular problem than preachers. We live by our reputations. So often there is the tendency to want to artificially be this, that, or the other. But Christ, the one we follow, made himself of no reputation.

The Practice: Courage

The second characteristic cited was courage. Do you remember the cowardly lion of the *Wizard of Oz?* He found it difficult to live without a little bit of courage. Most people do. But the Scripture teaches that the ability to have courage is built in. It's a part of our life. Many people haven't learned how to tap it, how to find it, how to employ it, and haven't had the encouragement of having been courageous at some point in their life.

Trust God

First, learn to trust God to help you be courageous. Paul said, "I can do all things through Christ which strengtheneth me" (Phil. 4:13, KJV). Well then, you can be courageous in Christ. Let God provide that which you need. Try to imagine a situation where courage would be required. You say, "Wow, I could never pull that off. I could never have courage in that situation." But, perhaps, you could. God seldom provides it in advance. You have to draw on it when you need it.

Avoid Presumption

Secondly, learn to distinguish between bravado, presumption, and courage. He is not calling you to punch out your chest and say to the world, "I'm a brave man (or woman)." Nor is God calling you to get up on a balcony and jump to impress someone with how softly you will land by his help. Jesus resisted that. He called it presumption. Courage is quieter. Courage responds to battles the world sometimes doesn't know are being joined.

Broaden Your Application

That leads to a third suggestion. Learn to discover the courageous act in every area of life. We think of courage as something that goes on in the battlefield, on the sickbed, in some kind of personal encounter, or, perhaps, in some political arena. But courage is needed in more subtle moments such as when a tremendous cloud of depression settles over you. Courage resists the cloud, continues to function, and affirms God's faithfulness. Courage may be called for in a situation when you are up against something that nobody else is ever going to know you were up against, and they're not going to be able to give you credit, even if you do well. But it calls for courage, and you will know it. Courage has to do with standing firm when people are assaulting your personhood or your reputation and you think you have every right to react. Courage is Christlike.

The Practice: Compassion

Now let me offer three actions for compassion. Jesus was such a compassionate person that throughout the verses of Scripture related to his life, we find him expressing compassion and responding to need. He saw a group of hungry and tired people and he had compassion toward them. A leper came and he had compassion and reached out and touched him. A woman mourned her dead son; he had compassion. There appeared a blind man; he had compassion. To be Christlike is to have compassion.

Trust New Instincts

Do you remember the discussion on this subject? I said, "In Christ, compassion is natural." For your first action, learn to trust your new nature with its instincts to help. You will want to help. It takes worldly training to make yourself invulnerable to other people's needs and to protect yourself from those needs. But your new instinct as a Christian will be to help. Trust it. Reach out. So you get your hands slapped, and so they don't appreciate it? That's not your problem. You are to respond as Christ responded.

Serve Others

Secondly, in an effort to be compassionate, seek to serve other people's needs and not your needs. So often we can, even in our goodness to other people, get to where we are really only meeting our needs. We're building our reputation again. Or we're trying so hard to protect our right to serve someone that we won't let them stand on their own two feet. One of the problems in society is how to respond compassionately to people less fortunate, in whatever area of the world or of life, without robbing them of their self-respect. Make sure you are serving them and not yourself.

Persist

Thirdly, if you want to be Christlike and develop compassion, learn persistence. Compassion breeds demands. It's easy to get discouraged. You try to help people, and they turn out to be unlovely. Perhaps, that's how they got in trouble in the first place. Their demands and unloveliness will tempt you to lose heart. But the real blessing, the real sense of having been a part of what God is about in that situation, comes when you stay with it. The good Samaritan didn't say, "Gee whiz, fellow, that's tough. I feel for you," and walk on. He did something about it. He not only bound up his wounds, but he also helped him to a place where he could recuperate. Then he provided for the ongoing process of recuperation. Persist. I remember with shame the many times I tried to talk my wife out of working with a young shampoo girl with whom she labored for several years. I said, "Forget it, honey. She will never change." And the drama of that girl's new life continues to amaze me. I was wrong. Stay with compassion's demands.

The Practice: Spirituality

Spirituality was the fourth trait cited. Let me offer suggestions to help you in this area.

Spiritual Priorities

Seek first the kingdom of God and his righteousness. It's a matter of priorities. So often our priorities are fouled up, and that's the reason we make such dumb decisions. We're not working off of a clear-cut sense of priorities. Jesus spoke so plainly to that. "Seek ye first," he said, "the kingdom of God and his righteousness; and all these things shall be added unto you" (Matt. 6:33, KJV). He says, "I know you have need of the things that cause your stomach to growl or cause you to be cold or cause you to hurt, but seek ye first the kingdom of God." If we are to be spiritual as Christ was spiritual, then we will put the kingdom of God and his righteousness first.

Regular Prayer

Secondly, meet him regularly in prayer. Call on him. The ability to commune with God is absolutely necessary to being Christlike and to having the spirituality that marked his life unlike any other life that has ever trod this earth. I saw a cartoon one time of a man in prayer. In the second frame he wasn't saying anything, but just doing exactly the same thing. In the third frame he was still in that particular position, hands folded, head bowed, only this time he said, "Yes, I understand that." Then in the next frame, he sat quietly again. In the last frame, he was looking at somebody kind of surprised, and he said, "He put me on hold." That's all right. Maybe he has us on hold for a purpose. Maybe that's part of the process. In fact, Romans 5 talks about patience being a part of that which develops character. But don't let a sense of being on hold keep you from regular, heartfelt, honest-to-God prayer.

Practice Presence

Thirdly, practice the presence of God. Believe in his indwelling presence. If you've asked him to come live in your life, it doesn't matter how long it's been since you affirmed that fact. He's in your life in the presence of his Spirit, just waiting for you to release him, to let him begin to work in you. If you would imitate the one he sent to show us the way as well as to redeem us from our sins, you would find that process accelerating beyond belief. If you are in Christ, this is God's purpose for you. He's given you the power, and life is the process. If you're not, there's no way you can do what I've been talking about. You are powerless. You are completely unable to imitate him successfully or to enter into that God-ordered process by which you are remade. It can only be accomplished in terms of an indwelling Christ. God says his salvation is free to whosoever will invite him in. When you do, the process can begin.

Summary

As you imitate him, let tiny steps of progress be cause for praise, and learn to rejoice in all things. God is the one at work in you. You are simply trying to cooperate in the process.

Part III
THE INSTRUCTION OF THE SPIRIT

11 The Role of Difficulties

I am committed to the idea that Christians grow through difficulty. Yet many of us have found our lives too superficial, our Christian understanding too shallow, to deal with some of the things that have come our way. Too many Christians seem to fall by the wayside because they lack the necessary spiritual strength. The harder they try, the harder they seem to fall. Is there a process, a secret to growth and victory? If there is a secret, I believe it is understanding the role of difficulties in the Christian life and being sensitive to the "instruction of the Spirit" that God has provided each disciple of the Lord Jesus Christ in such difficulties.

The words *instruction of the Spirit* need clarification. In John 14:16-17 Jesus promised his disciples that he would "pray the Father, and he shall give you another Comforter, that he may abide with you forever; even the Spirit of truth" (KJV). He further explained in verse 26, "But the Comforter, which is the Holy Ghost, whom the Father will send in my name, he shall teach you all things" (KJV). As explained in the early pages of this book, God has not left us to our own resources in our discipleship, but he has given us his own indwelling presence, his Holy Spirit. The Spirit is Christ in our lives. He is the power and the person by which the image of Christ, according to the intent of the Father, is recreated in our lives.

The context in which this is done, the laboratory in which we are made over, is the sum of our days, and so Paul said in Romans 8:28-29, "We know that all things work together for good to them that love God, to them who are the called according to his purpose" (KJV). Does this include the painful problems and difficulties that beset us? The witness of Scripture is a resounding yes! In the midst of this we know the presence, power, and gentle instruction of the Spirit.

For centuries believers have drawn solace and encouragement in their walk with its various trials from the example of the Israelites during their wilderness journey. In the time that elapsed between their deliverance from Egypt's bondage and their possession of the Promised Land, they were transformed by their trials and trained by their difficulties from a motley group of slaves to a mighty, obedient host. God's own presence in the form of a cloud by day and pillar of fire by night led them.

In the same way, he leads us through the wilderness of our earthly pilgrimage, but with a purpose—that we might be conformed to the image of his Son. Few passages speak more directly to this process than those found in Romans 5:1-5.

> Therefore being justified by faith, we have peace with God through our Lord Jesus Christ: By whom also we have access by faith into this grace wherein we stand, and rejoice in hope of the glory of God. And not only so, but we glory in tribulations also: knowing that tribulation worketh patience; And patience, experience; and experience, hope: And hope maketh not ashamed; because the love of God is shed abroad in our hearts by the Holy Ghost which is given unto us" (KJV).

This passage begins with a restatement of our condition in Christ. There are too many people confused about what it means to belong to the Christ, about what it means to be saved, about what the Scripture means when it talks about salvation. Many in the church also reflect some confusion about this. People outside the church have not only confusion but often caricature and misinformation. These first two verses speak directly to it. "Therefore, since we are justified by faith . . ." (v. 1). Because of our belief, we have been justified in God's sight. Let me define "justified" in a rather elementary, but I hope effective, way by putting the words "never sinned" at the end of the word—justified never sinned. Say it rapidly and it sounds as if you are saying, "just as if I had never sinned." Now, that's what "justified" means. It means that God, as we receive Jesus Christ and his death on the cross into our lives, accepts us as if we had never sinned. You may say, "That's not right. I have sinned. I've rebelled before God." That's true. But Jesus Christ came to make us whole again, to make us new again.

Our Immediate Blessings

There are two things that result from this relationship, this experience of being justified, which is another word for being saved or reclaimed or redeemed from the situation that has befallen us because of our rebellion. The first is that we have peace with God through our Lord Jesus Christ. Now, this concept of peace with God is not the peace that you have between two warring parties that come together and negotiate a settlement. Not at all. It's a peace you have when a rebellious subject comes and surrenders himself completely to his sovereign.

So many of us don't want peace with God unless we can negotiate something that will fit our situation and allow us to keep on doing some of the things we know we ought to quit. One day I was listening to a commentator talk about an international conflict. He said one of the groups had talked about negotiated peace. But he said that usually the person who starts talking about a negotiation is the person who is in danger of losing. I think that may be true of people negotiating with God.

We must come to God and say, "God, I have sinned. I have failed you. I have rebelled." When we come to make peace on those terms, then we have peace that is enduring. We are no longer estranged from God. We are no longer at war with God. But there is a peace that passeth all understanding as we come back to God.

Now the second thing in justification is that not only do we have this peace with God, but we also have something called "access by faith." It's like walking through a door. We have access to a very special place. Let's use these terms—a place called grace. This is a place where we have forgiveness and God receives us and counts us as one of his children. We walk through the door into a place of forgiveness and belonging to God and being his child, "in which we stand" (Rom. 5:2, RSV).

How different this is from the concept of salvation that provides only for the by-and-by and the when-I-quit-breathing stage of things. Salvation is a present reality. The word *stand* has to do with something you are doing now. It's your standing before God, and it's a place of grace, love, and acceptance. Our churches ought to reflect this. The church ought to be a place where, above all other places, you can be accepted and forgiven and loved and cared for because that reflects the place called grace where God receives us and wherein we stand. Let us rejoice in this place of grace. Standing here now, let us rejoice in the hope of God.

But the hope of the glory of God nurtures our future, too. Now, if you will think about it, we have three time zones: past, present, and future. Each of these has been taken care of in this situation. We've been justified by faith; God has wiped out our past. He's counted our sin and our rebellion as nothing because of what Jesus Christ has done for us. We are standing in a place of grace. He is dealing with our present. And we glory in the hope, or rejoice in the hope, of the glory of God. He has taken care of our future.

Time to Grow

In this situation, God has provided for our growth in a very beautiful way. He's made provision for us not just to stand still but to grow, to become. I used to look at the children in my congregation in Knoxville. I was so aware that in a few years they would look quite different. Someday they would be grown and sitting there with their own husbands or wives and children, and I would think, What will happen in the meantime? They'll change. They'll be molded by their circumstances. But so should we as Christians. God has provided a way for us to grow. This passage talks about God's plan to grow us.

Growth Through Tribulation

Verse 3 says, "More than that, we rejoice in our sufferings." You may want to confess, "Lord, I'm not so keen on that. What do you mean?" First of all, note the relationship to hope. We rejoice in the hope of the glory of God, but we also rejoice in something else. We rejoice in tribulations. These are related. The hope that we are moving toward is in process right now. And tribulations is not a word that means just sickness. It doesn't mean just suffering or even the various emotional and physical kinds of things that come upon us. It means any kind of stress or trial or problem—anything we have to cope with in life. So many people live in abject fear of what might happen. They live more or less cowering before what might be and trying to cover all bets against any possibility of tribulation coming into their lives. Here the Scripture says we need to rejoice in those tribulations. Why? Because God uses such events to grow us. Now, let's try to understand that.

We will experience tribulations. They are given. They have to do with the reality of a hostile, fallen world. Being a Christian does not make you immune to the problems of life. In fact, you often discover them with a new kind of intensity. But the idea here is that somehow tribulation "worketh patience." Now, that is the King James language. What it means is that being exposed to trials and problems, suffering of any kind in life, causes a certain process. Actually, the term "working" here could be used to describe a potter working clay. Have you ever been to a pottery shop and watched the potter at work? I could watch that for hours—the coordination of the hands and feet, the spinning of the wheel. But I've noticed that the potter is always working the clay. This is the truth here. Tribulations work us like that.

Endurance

But what is it working toward? The word is "patience." Now, again, that is a King James word that might mean more to us if we substituted the word *endurance* as used in the Revised Standard Version. Trials work endurance. They work a certain toughness into our lives, a certain ability to stand before come-what-may. A lot of us don't want this process to go on. It's hard to encourage, and I'm not sure that we're all that excited about it. But if we could come to see it as the process by which we not only learn to cope but also by which we become what God wants us to be, then we wouldn't have to rebel in events, tough as they might be. We could see God at work in them.

It helps to remember scriptural truths. They, too, are part of the "instruction of the Spirit." In 1 Corinthians 10 there is a Scripture I memorized as a young man, and I can't tell you how much it has helped me. "No temptation has overtaken you that is not common to man. God is faithful, and he will not let you be tempted beyond your strength." In the midst of circumstances that you think will crush you, you need to hang on to that verse. God will not allow you to be confronted with more than you are able to endure. "But with the temptation will also provide the way of escape, that you may be able to endure it."

The first truth is that this is a part of the common lot of men. But the second truth is that God is aware of you in this situation. He knows what you can handle.

The second thing we need to understand is found in John 16:33.

Jesus said, "In the world you have tribulation." "Lord, how well we know that!" We don't have to live long to see and testify to that out of our own scar tissue. But then Jesus says, "Be of good cheer, I have overcome the world." What did he mean by that? Recall again Romans 8:28, this time in the RSV. "We know that in everything God works for good with those who love him, who are called according to his purpose." Now, this is what has happened. Satan has come upon us with all of these tribulations. These are his plans, his efforts, a part of the fallen environment in which we live, to bring us down and crush us. But God has turned the tables on him in terms of the Christian life. He takes these same events which Satan has designed to crush us and uses them to grow us. "Be of good cheer, I have overcome the world." So, in Romans 8:28 we find that all things—tribulations, trials, even blessings—are part of God's effort to grow us. They work together for good. God is not the author of evil. You need to hear that. James 1:13-14 makes that clear. These are not events that God lays on you. God doesn't zap you (to use the language of the modern idiom) with such events; but God does allow them. He allows them because he is soveriegn over all things. In the permissive will of God there is no surrender of God's sovereignty in such events. He will use them for the instruction of the Spirit. And the process is one in which you can grow.

In Hebrews we find these words: "Looking to Jesus, the pioneer and perfecter of our faith" (12:2). Jesus is the one who is doing this work in us. "Who for the joy that was set before him endured the cross, despising the shame." That means he disregarded the shame. He didn't even count it a problem. Many times Christians are in situations that cause them to be ashamed, but that is strictly a worldly feeling. Jesus didn't worry about the fact that the cross was a social disaster. He was looking at the joy set before him of doing the will of God, and he endured it. And what we are to try to find in tribulation is the ability to endure.

Let me use the analogy of the body. When physiologists began to work with astronauts, one of the problems they anticipated early was peculiar to an astronaut in a weightless environment. You have seen pictures of the astronauts floating around inside their spaceships. They have a real problem there. They no longer have the reality of gravity. Gravity not only keeps us down and makes us come down when we go up, but gravity is a part of something we are working against all the time. Our bodies are maintaining their strength and their facility to function based on that working. When the body is not used, it atrophies. The scientists knew that astronauts, in a weightless environment, would have both muscular and bone deterioration. In fact, they have measured such deterioration. So they've had to develop artificial ways that astronauts could work their bodies because they know bodies have to be worked to maintain fitness. And they know that the bodies grow against tension and work. You can put someone in bed for a while and when they get up they're very weak. So the scientists designed an exercise program for the astronauts that would give their bodies something to work against.

Experience: The Instruction of the Spirit

Our new life is like that. It grows as it is pitted against the tensions and the tribulations of life. So Paul says we can glory in tribulations, knowing that they work endurance. And endurance does something else—endurance works experience. Now, the word *experience* here could also be translated "character." It refers to somebody who has confidence. But it literally means people who know because they have walked through something that they can live through. As mentioned earlier, my wife has had a tremendous ministry to other people who are dealing with eye problems because she'd been there. And the greatest words in the world are, "I know how you feel." It encourages somebody when they know that another has been there first. But one of the things I think we fail to realize is that when we have come through something, we subsequently stand a little stronger, with a little more confidence and with less fear in our lives. This is what the Scripture means when it says, "endurance produces character." (Undoubtedly, this is the truth Paul described in more personal terms in 2 Corinthians 12:7 ff.)

I read a story recently of a group that climbed the Grand Teton Mountains in Wyoming in the winter. It's extremely dangerous, not only because of the cold but also because of the possibility of avalanches and hypothermia. One of the young ladies who made the climb was from the East. She came back from the climb and was interviewed by a writer. He found her glowing. He said to her, "Why did you do this? Why did you take this chance and put yourself in such a difficult situation?" And she said, "Well, I'm a person who is overloaded with anxiety and fear, and I felt that if I could somehow do something like this, it would give me courage for living." And, in fact, it did. But we don't have to go to the Tetons. We don't have to find some great, dangerous event to take on. Life presents the kinds of trials and tribulations that God knows you need. We don't have to go around ordering a set that we think will take care of our weak muscles. We just live day by day and find those things that we need to work endurance. And the endurance will, under the instruction of the Spirit, work the experience that we need in order to have new strength and new confidence in our ability to live.

One day I was parked on the ramp at the Nashville Flying Service calling the Weather Bureau to find out what the weather was in Knoxville. At that point it was zero-zero at McGhee-Tyson Field and illegal to land, not to mention unwise. I was waiting for the fog to lift to at least instrument minimums. I couldn't make a legal attempt until conditions had risen to 400 feet and one mile. When I got the word that it had risen to that level, I took off for Knoxville. I confess, I was a bit anxious because I hadn't been flying enough to keep my proficiency to the point where I could go into that kind of situation without a bit of uneasiness. As I flew on top of the clouds, I went over all of the procedures in my mind. But there was another fellow also on top of the clouds in a bit of trouble. Departure Control asked me to relay messages to him. It was great for me. I quit worrying about myself when I got involved in trying to help him. That's a lesson, isn't it? When you're in the midst of your own problems and think you're drowning in them, try helping somebody else. You may find that it not only helps you take care of your problems but also that you have a sense of well-being for trying to help somebody else.

By the time I got to Knoxville, the weather began to lift and I had no trouble making the approach. Later it occurred to me that my problem was a lack of experience. Oh, I had all the ratings and the required time in my log book, but I was short on recent experience which brings the kind of confidence you need in such a situation. Now, that's what we receive in life through tribulations when we allow the Spirit to instruct us and grow us. They bring confidence to our lives. It's part of the process of being conformed to the image of God's Son. It's not just the process of growing stronger, but it's growing stronger in a certain direction.

Nineteen hundred seventy-five was one of the most interesting years of my life. As I look back on it, I'd have to say it was one of the best years of my life. Yet it was a year that started off with my wife blind in one eye. Surgery that we prayed would help seemingly had failed, and we didn't know how long the other eye would hold. It was a year in which I suddenly found myself struggling with the question of where God wanted me to be after fifteen years of being settled into a position that was important to me and in which I felt great joy. And when I felt sure Knoxville was where God wanted me, I trembled at the reality of it. It meant breaking away from our home of fifteen years in Richmond. It meant moving high school kids to Knoxville at one of the roughest periods in which to ask children to adjust. It meant moving at a time when we knew we were going to have to face additional surgery for Dot. It meant being separated. It meant the anxiety of a new job. (This experience is discussed again in the chapter on stress.)

We tackled the anxiety. We tackled the separation. We tackled surgery. There had been difficulties among relatives that we were caught up in and anxious about. Yet I tell you that it was one of the best years of my life. Why? Because I quickly became aware that God was at work in my life, blessing me, strengthening me, and giving me a new ability to endure. And out of the endurance came experience. I'm still a neophyte; each new year reminds me I'm still a child in what's happening. But I thank God it is happening. It's the instruction of the Spirit, and it helps me understand the role of difficulties.

12 Dealing with Sin

In 1973, the world-famous physician, Dr. Karl Menninger of the clinic by the same name, shocked both the psychiatric world and the theological world by publishing a book with the title, *Whatever Became of Sin?* In this book, Dr. Menninger made a candid effort both to warn his own profession of their limitations and to awaken mine to our negligence. He felt that he needed to call attention to a problem within our society. The problem was that in our efforts to rid society of wrong, we have simply begun eliminating the things we call wrong. Our attempts were more than efforts to decriminalize such things as the smoking of marijuana. They were efforts to "de*sin*ize," you might say—things that have plagued and corrupted and degraded and diminished man from the beginning of time. In his book, Dr. Menninger sounded more like a preacher page by page. He implied that we must learn to equate moral health and mental health. We must face up to our sin, confess it, seek forgiveness for it, and turn from it, whether you call it repentance or what. If not, he warned, in the process of simply changing the name, we're going to end up deeper in despair when what we need so badly is repair.

When someone starts talking about sin, there's much confusion. People inherently feel that there is some kind of relativism in force that frees them of much of what is called sin. What has God revealed to his own to steer them from such confusion?

First, in James 4:17, we find that: "To him that knoweth to do good and doeth it not, to him it is sin" (KJV). There is, deep in the heart of every created individual, a kind of implanted law which seems to be learned in every culture, regardless of race and ties of information, knowledge, or ethical concepts. The violation of this deep sense of right and wrong works out into a universal experience that people try in a myriad of different ways to explain away. Yet as the *Dictionary of Ethics* says, "The similarities in these codes of conduct in diverse cultures indicates a common moral heritage for all mankind which neither materialism nor naturalism can explain away." Sin is a common understanding.

There are five classic views as to the source of these codes of conduct. There's the subjective view which says simply that it is the highest idea a man holds about himself. This becomes the inner code, the inner ethical constraint, against which he works. When he is in harmony with it, he feels good. When he's in disharmony with it, he feels troubled.

Then there is the collective view. This view says it is not an individual's idea. It's, rather, an accumulation of the highest thoughts that men have ever had about what it means to be a human being.

There is the utilitarian thought. This is the thought that is gaining such wide acceptance in our time. It says simply that the sense of right, the code of conduct which we are to respond to, is that conduct which generates the greatest good for the greatest number. That sounds find, doesn't it? But what if you're not among the greatest number? What if you are a minority, and somebody is working out a utilitarian concept of what's right, but you're one of those few people for whom it is wrong?

Then there is the divine notion. This is the concept that indeed God is not only the progenitor of man's history, but he is involved in man's history by his ongoing constraints, by his law, and by his divine direction. And as man bucks and revolts against it, he finds himself increasingly alienated from himself, others, and God.

But there is one thing upon which man is increasingly able to agree. Despite his efforts to limit the number of things he is willing to call sin, there is rarely a person who will not agree with Romans 3:23 when it says, "All have sinned, and come short of the glory of God" (KJV). So the question, as Menninger pointed out, is not "Whatever became of sin?" Sin is with us. Nothing has become of it. It is there, flourishing malignantly under the verbage with which we try in vain to bury it. The problem is what shall we do about it? What shall we do about sin?

Let me point out, however, I'm not talking about other people's sin. I'm not talking about social sin. I'm not talking about those things that haunt us as a society and call us to action, as significant as that might be, whether it be pornography or drugs or prostitution or perversion or embezzlement or crime or poverty or oppression or exploitation of any kind. I'm talking about another kind of sin.

I'm talking about my sin and your sin—the sin that besets the believer. What shall we do about our sin?

You say, "Wait a minute. Isn't that what the good news is all about? Isn't that what Christianity is all about?" Yes, it is. In Jesus Christ, God is dealing with our sin. Sin has estranged us. All religious efforts in every culture are simply an effort to overcome the alienation people instinctively feel. But God cut right through our religion with Jesus Christ to establish his own bridge to reconcile us. He deals with our sin not only by letting Jesus die for it, not only by forgiving us and cleansing us, but also by enabling us to live a different kind of life. Yes, that's what the good news is all about.

I talked with a young seminarian one time. He said, "I've lost my way." He said, "Somewhere in the process of trying to learn how to minister, I've lost my way." I said, "What do you mean?" He said, "For instance, I'm ready to graduate, and I don't have any good news to tell anybody." I said to him, "You have lost your way because above anything else you've been called to do, you have been called to preach good news—the good news that God was in Christ reconciling man to himself, the good news that Romans 6:23 spells out: 'For the wages of sin is death, but the free gift of God is eternal life in Christ Jesus our Lord.' "

But the real problem we face as Christians is what do we do about our tendency to continue to sin after that fact? We have accepted Jesus Christ. We have embraced the fact that Jesus Christ was on that cross, not for generic man but for particular persons. The problem is that sin persists.

In the eighth chapter of John lies that wonderful passage in which Jesus comes upon a crowd preparing to stone a woman to death. She had been caught in the very act of adultery and brought to the town square. The people were picking up stones with which they would crush her life in retribution. Jesus walked into their midst and said simply, "Let the one in your midst without sin cast the first stone." You know the story. No one could do it. They dropped their stones and walked away. No one could throw that first rock because there was no one there who could deny his own sin. But that's not the whole story. Jesus then turned to the woman and said, "No man condemns you, and neither do I. Go, sin no more."

But we do sin. And the burden that most Christians feel today is the result of continuing to sin. Since our new birth, we have written a record of failure again and again. It has robbed us of the joy and the faith and the victory of which Scripture speaks so eloquently as the individual Christian's heritage. And for some, it constitutes a loss of heart.

Once, while preaching on the theme, a young man came in from off the streets. He heard these words. It was as if he were transfixed. And at the close of the service, he made a public commitment. I realized that here was an individual who had not just lost heart because of the sin that had come since he had become a Christian—he had felt as if he no longer belonged to the Lord. Suddenly, he heard the word that called him back. He heard the instruction of the Spirit.

We do sin. We sin again and again. Yet in 1 John we read: "My little children, these things write I unto you, that ye sin not. And if any man sin, we have an advocate with the Father, Jesus Christ the righteous" (2:1, KJV). The first part of that verse says we can sin. The second part of the verse says we do sin. The question is, "What can we do about it?"

The Spirit provides a way to deal with it. That's what the Christian life is all about. It's about dealing with sin, about letting God remake us through the power of the indwelling Christ, about letting him help us to triumph over those sins that beset us, and about learning to walk and live in a different way. We can deal with our continuing sin.

Many think that God has simply left them helpless in the Christian experience and that their only hope is for heaven. They think that one of these days it will be all right, and they'll be lifted out of the slime and mud that they have instinctively returned to no matter how many times they've had nobler ideas.

Let's take a look at the kind of sin that besets Christians. First of all, there is the sudden kind. "Therefore let any one who thinks that he stands take heed lest he fall." Maybe you are familiar with that passage in 1 Corinthians 10:12. I have to remind myself again and again of this possibility.

In flying, we have an old saying: "When you're fat and happy, look out." When the engines are purring and the instruments all seem to be right where they ought to be, and the weather looks great, and everything seems to be perfect, look out. I don't know how many times I've suddenly awakened from that thought and started scanning instruments to try to find out if there wasn't something wrong somewhere. I listen and look and cross-check. We need to do that in the Christian life. About the time we think we've got it made, we find ourselves taking the biggest fall of all. Sin has a way of coming upon us like that.

Secondly, we experience sin as the product of meditation. It's premeditated sin. It's the kind of thing that comes into our lives first as an idea. But it is nurtured and allowed to flourish. Then it flowers. James 1:14 says: "But each person is tempted when he is lured and enticed by his own desire. The desire, when it has conceived gives birth to sin." Many Christians invite that kind of problem. They let notions remain in their heads until there is a rooting and flowering. The result is something of which they would not have thought they were capable. Sin can emerge just that way.

The point that President Jimmy Carter was trying to make following his *Playboy* interview is that the kind of thing that you allow to go on in your heart has the potential to find its way into your life.

Sin can be sudden or premeditated. But sin can also be habitual. Perhaps this is our biggest problem. In Romans 7:17, Paul says, "So then it is no longer I that do it, but sin which dwells within me." Your life can, after a time, be programmed to where sin comes as natural as getting up and going to bed. And when you become a Christian, if you don't let Christ begin to reprogram you, the habits of a lifetime will continue to trip you up. You say to yourself, "I couldn't do this kind of thing if I were a Christian. I couldn't be a Christian, or I wouldn't think that way." But you can. You can allow the habits of a lifetime to continue to dominate you. Or worse, you can allow new habits of exploiting people, of hurting people, of entertaining thoughts of hardness and evil and anger and revenge in your heart until it becomes a way of life.

Every now and then I come across people who have a sharp way of speaking, a hard way of speaking. They tend to cut people, but they are not aware of it. They don't know how they sound. They don't hear how that sounds to the other person, nor do they see the internal wince and hurt and estrangement that results. It's simply a habit.

Whether suddenly or premeditatedly or habitually, we sin. What does God provide to deal with it? This passage in 1 John is, perhaps, one of the most classic in all of the Scripture for helping an individual deal with his sin.

> My little children, these things write I unto you, that ye sin not. And if any man sin, we have an advocate with the Father, Jesus Christ the righteous: And he is the propitiation for our sins: and not for ours only, but also for the sins of the whole world. And hereby we do know that we know him, if we keep his commandments. He that saith, I know him, and keepeth not his commandments, is a liar, and the truth is not in him. But whoso keepeth his word, in him verily is the love of God perfected: hereby know we that we are in him. He that saith he abideth in him ought himself also so to walk, even as he walked (2:1-6, KJV).

What resources do we have? First of all, we have forgiveness. Listen: "My little children, these things write I unto you that you sin not. And if any man sin, shame on him." No, that's not what it says. "And if any man sin, I will zap him." That's not what it says either. That's just the way you feel. Does it say, "And if any man sins, the church will kick him out"? They don't. Maybe they should, but they don't. No, it says, "And if any man sin, we have an advocate with the Father, Jesus Christ the righteous: And he is the propitiation for our sins." Do you know what it's saying? If we sin, God has provided forgiveness.

We don't like that. We don't trust forgiveness. Those of you who are parents understand what I mean. Your children break your rules. "Mama, Daddy, forgive me." You want to, but you know if you do, they'll do it again. You feel you can't trust the little buggers. Wait a minute. You're already in trouble. You not only have child-rearing problems, but you also have God-fearing problems. You are saying to yourself, "I don't believe God can forgive me because if he forgives me, I'll do the same thing again." You're also saying, "If I let God forgive me, I'll do the same thing again. Therefore, I won't let God forgive me." If there's one thing this book teaches, and if there's one thing that the life of Jesus Christ spells out in a way we cannot deny, it is that there is in forgiveness a power to change beyond all of our little punishments, beyond all of our little restraints, beyond all of our little penances. There is a power in forgiveness to change.

To me the first and primary resource God gives us for dealing with sin is forgiveness. You say, "But surely there is an end to his patience! I exhausted it somewhere way, way back there. I'm all out of my right to forgiveness. He forgave me the first 1,823 times I did that, and I haven't had the heart since then to ask him." But the Scripture implies that he forgives over and over and over and over and over.

But that's not the only resource God provides us for our sin. He provides dynamics for change. First, as we read this passage, we run into the words "these things write I unto you." This refers to his Word. It refers to the guidance he's given us. Once on a backpacking trip, I backtracked to my car to get a flashlight after starting up a mountain becuse I knew I was going to need that light during the night. I was going to be moving through places with which I was not familiar. I needed the light. It wouldn't light up the whole mountain. It wouldn't show me the way all the way down. But it would help me make my way step by step. The Scripture is that kind of light. We have guidance. If we would open our hearts to what God is trying to say to us in his Word, we would find increasing strength and wisdom for dealing with the sin in our lives.

Secondly, this passage implies there is a resource in Christian fellowship. The importance of other Christians in helping us overcome sin is critical. Alcoholics Anonymous is still, as far as I'm concerned, the number one successful way to deal with alcoholism. Why is that? First, because it helps the addict look beyond himself. It causes him to look up to God and reach for help that he can't find in himself. But they also relate the alcoholic to other people who have the same problem. Together they strengthen and encourage each other.

This is what the church does. You say, "Now, I'm not so sure I've been in one of those churches. The churches I've gone to, you can't admit that you sin. You have to put on a false face and act as if you're perfect." One of the things a church should admit regularly is that it is composed of sinners saved by grace. Christians are people in pilgrimage. They should be a people increasingly aware of their faults and increasingly aware of what God is trying to do in their midst to help them overcome. Christians need each other. Only as we begin to let our fellow believers accept us as we are and encourage us and strengthen us on our pilgrimage do we really begin to overcome.

A third aspect of God's provision is the indwelling reality of his own Son. Jesus said, "I send you another comforter." The word he used meant "Just like me." Again he said, "I will not leave you alone. I will come to you." And he wasn't talking about the second coming. He was talking about his own indwelling presence.

As mentioned in chapter 2, the Scripture talks about a strange paradox. It says, "Abide in me." Christ is saying, "Make your house in me. Make your life in me." Then he adds, "And I will abide in you." The indwelling Christ is also the Christ in whom we dwell. Pity the person who doesn't have some individual in his life or in his understanding who lives in such a way as to encourage and inspire them.

Yet Christ is the only sufficient model. He dwells within us to give us strength to follow him and to become like him. He is the enabler in our lives. And it's as we abide in him and follow him and imitate him that we begin to overcome the sins that plague us.

Finally, there is prayer. Daily, moment by moment, instantaneously, we can get in contact with God. It's like having a direct radio frequency to his presence. You can talk to him.

To show how prayer works, go back to the three kinds of sin that beset us as Christians: sudden, premeditated, habitual. Do you realize that the Lord's Prayer speaks directly to sudden sin? "Lead us not into temptation." You see, when we are walking daily with an awareness of our susceptibility, and when we are coming at each hour and each day and each situation with an awareness that we can blow it, we're less likely to do so because we are more likely to depend upon God.

Secondly, we talked about premeditated sin. Prayer helps Christ to help us do battle with the monster that sin can become in our lives. The Scripture says, "Resist the devil and he will flee from you" (Jas. 4:7). You can turn to God and ask him for the power to resist that one who would like to plant, nurture, and flower a great sin in your life.

Thirdly, we talked about habitual sin. The habit of prayer has a way of helping the believer to overcome would-be sin habits. The habit of trying to live the Christlike life is the habit that filters all others.

Cybernetics has opened up such an understanding of the human mind that we are confused about the computer and the brain. Is the computer a super brain, or is the brain a super model from which we develop computers? Either way, we are beginning to understand some interrelationships. Take programming. We realize that we can program a computer procedure. When we want to change one, we have to substitute something. Christ, in a new way, becomes our substitute "mind" or "program." As we wait on him daily in prayer, we find that "mind" of Christ.

I once watched a football player carry the ball on a running play. He broke through the line, breaking a tackle as he did. A linebacker took a shot at him, and you would have thought it was going to knock him out of the stadium. But he kept his balance, and in a minute he was running upright again. A cornerback hit him full on, and he came right out of that tackle. He stiff-armed another person who had caught up with him. He escaped a trap over on the sideline, and falling and stumbling as a final pursuer threw a tackle at him, he fell across the goal line. At that point, the one thing that impressed me, other than the fact that he was for the other team, was that he never lost sight of the goal.

God calls us to live in such a way that we never lose sight of what he is trying to do in our lives, to conform us to the image of his Son and to grow us up into what he wants us to be. We don't have to let sin sideline us. We don't have to let it rob us of the faith and confidence we need to realize God's promise and leadership. In the instruction of the Spirit, we can deal with it.

13 Dealing with Doubt

It seems inevitable that a Christian should have to grapple with doubt. If you haven't, thank God. But don't be smug. It's like the pilots who have not landed with their wheels still tucked up under the airplane. One of the most embarrassing and terrifying things a pilot can do is to forget to put his wheels down before he lands, and suddenly realize, with the horrible scrape of bare metal on the runway, that he is landing in a most embarrassing condition. To avoid this, he goes through elaborate rituals to remember with checklists or little acrostics. The acrostic I've used through the years is G.U.M.P. It reminds me of gas, undercarriage down and locked, mixture, and prop. I can say G.U.M.P. in my sleep. I will call it out two or three times before I land, and uninitiated passengers are convinced that I've flipped my lid. They don't realize that I'm trying to get us back safely. It's such a concern, however, that the old pros say there are only two kinds of pilots: those who *have* landed with their gear up, and those who *will* land with their gear up.

A similar statement could be made about doubt and the Christian. There are only two kinds of Christians: those who have had to grapple with doubt at some point, and those who will. Yet doubt is such an enemy of faith that we must take it very seriously. We need to understand both how it works and what it can do to us. It is also a place where we can discover the instruction of the Spirit.

The Ravages of Doubt

In James 1:1-8, the writer speaks graphically of the damage doubt can cause. Read the passage for yourself. It says, for instance, that doubt can rob you of the very blessings of God. "For let not that man think that he shall receive anything of the Lord" (Jas. 1:7, KJV). Why? Because the realization of our petitions comes through faith. When our whole effort is undermined by doubt and when our doubts discourage us from even coming to God's throne of grace, we are robbed of untold blessings.

This passage in James says the person who doubts is as one who is tossed like a wave, without a sense of direction. Doubt undermines that sense of purpose in life that is so tremendously important to a person who feels God has not only redeemed him but has redeemed him for a purpose.

In addition, doubt produces spiritual instability, a condition in which there is no "rooting or grounding." We must be rooted and grounded in love. The alternative leaves us vulnerable to every wind and whim.

This is what our Lord would have for us—that we would have a sense of direction in him, that we would be rooted and grounded and stable in him. Doubt undermines all of this.

Understanding Doubt

It is important to understand doubt. It's so easy to talk about doubt without ever coming to grips with its dynamics and the forms that it might take. When we do understand doubt, then we can understand the scriptural antidote. Don't misunderstand this. There is no antidote for doubt itself, but there is an antidote for succumbing to doubt. The Spirit can help you to cope with it.

Doubt manifests itself in many different forms, but the Scripture delineates at least three basic forms of doubt. You will want to check your own experience against these three different forms of doubt because you may have experienced one or all of them. And while you may have experienced some other kind of doubt, I think you will be surprised at how fully these three forms cover the spectrum of your spiritual experience.

Intellectual Doubt

The first kind of doubt is the intellectual or rational doubt. This is the realm where so many first encounter doubt. It involves both the willingness and the ability to believe the things of God, the claims of God. Many believers are constantly dealing with intellectual doubt. They grapple with so much new information, with so many systems of thought that seem to contradict and stand in opposition to the system that incorporates their faith and their understanding of what God has done in Jesus Christ, that they regularly have to gird up the loins of their minds (see 1 Pet. 1:13) and wrestle with doubt.

Baker James Cauthen, for many years the executive secretary of the Foreign Mission Board, and the subject of a biography that I wrote under a commission from the Foreign Mission Board, once shared with me how he felt when he took a pastorate in a university community in his early years. He said, "You know, I hadn't been a reprobate. I hadn't been a drunkard. I hadn't gone off and played the prodigal in socially obvious ways. But I had struggled with intellectual doubt." He said, "I had a tender place in my heart for those in that struggle." I think God does, too.

The twentieth chapter of John tells a most unusual story of Jesus' postresurrection days. Jesus had been seen by several of his disciples, and they came to one of the other disciples, Thomas, and said, "We have seen the Lord" (v. 25) Thomas said, "I won't believe it." He added, "Until I can put my fingers in his wounds, I will not believe it." And then Jesus appeared to him and let him do just that. Thomas said, "My Lord and my God" (v. 28). I think that is a classic example of intellectual or rational doubt. It often issues from an experience of having been "burned." Some people try to move out in an early stage of faith and seek the Lord for everything under the Christmas tree, and find that the Lord is rather selective about the kinds of prayers he grants. And they come out of it so disillusioned they don't want to try anymore. Thomas had seen his dreams of what he thought the Messiah was supposed to be crushed on a cross. He wasn't about to believe again without some very specific information to undergird it.

But we also find out something else about doubt in Thomas's experience. It is an act of the will. "I *will not* believe," he said. Many times we stand over in the midst of our intellectual or rational doubt and say to God, "I will not believe unless you do such and such."

It's like the Pharisees who came to Jesus and said, "Give us a sign." If you read the context of that question, you will find it appalling. They had just been a part of the feeding of the four thousand. They had the crumbs of a miracle on their fingers and were belching its reality when they asked for a sign. Sometimes we come cuddling our doubt, our backs up, saying, "I will not believe," and yet there are miracles and signs and evidences all around us. But the fact that the Lord dealt as he did with Thomas indicates that he understands. He's patient with us; he's longsuffering with us. But many times the answer to our doubts is more evident than we would assume.

Experiential Doubt

There is a second kind of doubt. I believe this one would be most evident in a story told in the fourteenth chapter of Matthew. The disciples had tried to cross the Sea of Galilee ahead of the Lord. A storm had come up, and soon they were fearful for their lives. Then Jesus appeared to them. They were almost as afraid of the appearance of Jesus walking on the water as they were of the storm. That is, with the exception of Peter. Peter responded with tremendous excitement and with a great surge of faith. He said, "Lord, . . . bid me come unto thee on the water. And he said, Come." (Matt. 14:28-29, KJV). And Peter stepped out on the water and began walking toward the Lord. Don't you know he was exhilarated by the experience? But all of a sudden he became aware of the waves, and he began to sink. "Lord, save me" (v. 30, KJV). And the Lord reached out and caught him and chided him, "O thou of little faith, wherefore didst thou doubt?" (v. 31, KJV).

Now, many of us experience doubt in the same way. I call it a kind of midcourse or experiential doubt. It's doubt that comes after we've believed, after we've received the Lord. We're in some experience where we are having to walk by faith. Then something happens. The waves of our experience get big, and we begin to doubt. We begin to sink, so to speak. I'll share this with you. Many times I've prayed for a situation to come about, felt that it had, and moved out into it. Then in the midst of it, I lose heart. I have had that experience many times. In the preparations of sermons, it almost inevitably happens. I'll have an idea I'm convinced is of the Lord; I'll move into the Word; I'll begin to understand the tremendous wealth of teaching that surrounds the idea; I'll get real excited; and then about halfway through it, I'll begin to lose heart. I think, I'll never develop this. I'll never bring it to a point that people will understand. I haven't written a book yet that I haven't lost heart about halfway through it. It just seems to be my lot to lose heart somewhere in the midst of such efforts. I get through only by the grace of God. I know people who do this every day in a hundred ways. I can identify with them. It's a midcourse or experiential doubt.

Maybe you have suffered experiential doubt in a different way. You find a special prayer answered. You say, "Thank you, Lord." Then doubt comes flooding in from the author of doubt. "You don't really think that's God's work, do you? You don't really feel that was divine intervention, do you? If you'll look around, you'll find that there's a very natural explanation for it."

C. S. Lewis, in his book, *The Screwtape Letters,* has a senior devil giving a junior devil a little bit of advice. He says (loosely paraphrased), "Listen, what you need to do with these Christians when they begin to pray is to wait and see what happens. If the Lord answers their prayer, move in at once and tell them that there is really a natural cause for it. It wasn't the Lord answering their prayer at all." He said, "We call that the old 'heads I win, tails you lose' strategy."

How many times have you faced it? There's an obvious answer to your prayer. You say, "Thank-you, Lord." But there's an alternative explanation. There's another possibility. Which will you believe? Many times I've prayed, "Lord, answer this prayer, and do it in such a way that there is no other explanation, and we'll all have to praise your name." You know what I'm really asking for? "Lord, don't make me have to have faith. Don't make me have to trust you. Zap me in such a way that I am cut off at the pass of doubt." Experiential doubt is a very prevalent form.

Relational Doubt

There's a third kind of doubt. It has to do with our very understanding of who we are in relation to the Lord Jesus Christ. The Scripture tells us that by faith we are sons of God, children of God. We are cleansed, made new, adopted into his family. Obviously, this only applies to those who have received Jesus Christ by faith as Lord and Savior. That's the only way we have promise of becoming a part of the family of God. That's a relational fact of faith, and you would think, I could never doubt that. Oh, yes, you can. I used to think when the psalmist said, "What is man, that thou art mindful of him?" (Ps. 8:4, KJV) that he was asking the biggest philosophical question that had ever been asked. In fact, I've used it to introduce two sermons dealing with the nature of man. But the other day, while reading that passage, I saw it in another light altogether. I saw in it the way I feel at times when doubt comes surging in one me. "What is man, that thou art mindful of him?" Who am I the God who sustains this universe, who is the creator of something that is bigger than my ability even to imagine it, would be mindful of me? This is a relational doubt. Maybe you don't doubt the substance of revelation. Maybe you don't doubt that God was in Christ reconciling the world unto himself. Maybe you don't doubt that through faith some can experience a new life. But you do doubt that he could care for, forgive, and affirm as his child the likes of you.

I don't know how many of you are addicted to the TV show, *The Waltons,* but I once saw an episode that I thought was very poignant. It seemed that one of the boys decided that he wasn't really a Walton after all, that he was bound to have been a foundling, that some disreputable people had birthed him and then left him on the Walton's doorstep, and that they had then taken him in as one of their own. This meant the Walton children weren't really his brothers and sisters, and Mother and Father Walton weren't really his mother and father. His doubts led him into a depression. Now, like a lot of these plots, it's one of those things that happens to many people. Children in families experience this kind of fear. And everybody rushes in to quickly reassure them. The Waltons did that. But it was only when John Boy took his brother down to the courthouse and started looking up the records that the doubts receded.

I've counseled people who have been Christians for years and then began to doubt their relationship to Christ. I have to look up the records with them. We have to open the Word of God and read the promises of God again for that relationship to be affirmed. You know, even Christ experienced this kind of doubt. "Oh, no. Maybe I have, but the Lord didn't." No? What do you think He meant when he said, "My God, my God, why hast thou forsaken me?" (Matt. 27:46,KJV). The Scripture says Jesus "was in all points tempted like as we are" (Heb. 4:15,KJV). The Scripture also says that he fully became our sin there on the cross. I believe that even meant taking up that sense of estrangement and doubt of relationship that is inherent in sin. He knows what it is to doubt.

The Instruction of the Spirit

What is the cure? What is the antidote? Well, first of all, we need to know that it is common to people. When you begin to doubt, stop thinking that you have lost your faith or that you have done some horrible wrong which has excluded you from the family of God. But do recognize that there are some causes of doubt that you can bring on yourself.

When we let things creep into our life and begin to do things that we know we shouldn't, it undermines our faith. Sometimes the best way to deal with doubt is to repent. Come before the Lord and confess. Say, "Lord, I realize I have strayed. I've turned away from you." Doubt can fly out the window rapidly in moments like this because you are affirming again the reality of forgiveness.

The answer to doubt, however, is faith. You say, "That doesn't sound right. You say that when you don't have enough faith, you have doubt; but the answer to doubt is faith." That's what I'm saying. The answer to doubt is to believe God. You say, "That's my problem. I have trouble believing God." All right, the Scripture has an answer for that. In Romans 10:17, we read: "So then faith cometh by hearing, and hearing by the word of God" (KJV). In other words, the Bible says that as we claim the promises of God, as we come to understand the revelation of God throughout history, as we come to understand the purposes of God for us and for our church, our faith is strengthened. One of the miracles of all time, as far as I'm concerned, is that our doubts about the Scripture are almost readily strengthened by the study of the Scripture. As you come to understand what God would say to you, the Spirit of God uses the whole experience to instruct you and strengthen your heart and life.

There is another dimension to this. Faith flourishes in the family of faith. Many try to survive off by themselves, outside of an environment of believing, loving, caring people. It's like an ember trying to survive when it's kicked away from the main fire. We wonder where the glow goes. We wonder where the warmth goes. We wonder why we quit burning. The answer is that we were made to be a part of a larger environment. C. S. Lewis, the great English philosopher and Christian witness, said that he never really had to grapple with doubt until he was away from home in a strange hotel room. He discovered something very important. He discovered how necessary it is for us to be with people who can affirm our faith and with whom and from whom our faith can draw strength and reference. Many wonder why, when they get into a completely unbelieving environment, a scoffing, denying environment, they have to cope with doubt. The answer is self-evident. That does not mean that the Lord will not lead us into such places. That does not mean that these moments will not become places of witness and ministry for us. But it does mean that we need each other. The fellowship that is represented by a worship service or by Sunday School is critical to our lives. That passage of Scripture which says, "Not forsaking the assembling of ourselves together" (Heb. 10:25, KJV) has been quoted over and over again to strengthen Sunday School attendance. So some of us have assumed that was what God was talking about—raising the averages. Not at all. He's talking about our survival. He's talking about how much we need each other. (Chapter 4 dealt more in depth with this need.)

When Doubt Becomes Strength

Some of you have already grappled with doubt; some are now grappling with doubt; and some will grapple with future doubt. Whether it's the intellectual kind of doubt with the facts of faith, or the experiential kind of doubt with your own experience, or as you look about you and try to understand the people of God or even the purposes of God, or whether it has to do with your own relationship to God in Jesus Christ, you must affirm anew that you do believe and ask God to help you. I take great encouragement from the man who said to Jesus, "I believe; help thou mine unbelief" (Mark 9:24, KJV). Build your faith through the Word of God, and allow your faith to flourish in the midst of the people of God. Let the Spirit instruct you in the midst of your doubt.

Satan designs doubt to undermine our faith. He knows what it can do to us. The victory of God in the world is that he can take this same doubt when we overcome it through faith and let it become a source of new strength for us. This is what the Scripture means when it says, "Knowing this, that the trying of your faith worketh patience. But let patience have her perfect work, that ye may be perfect and entire, wanting nothing." (Jas. 1:3-4, KJV).

14 Dealing with Fear

Have you ever been afraid? Really afraid? If so, I can honestly say I know how you feel.

I have been afraid in different situations and for different reasons. I have known fear as a stomach-gnawing physical experience. I have known it as a mind-torturing kind of morbidity. A fear of my own death as anxiety over minor ailments would escalate into a mortal dread. I've known it in moments of sheer terror. I have known fear. I can identify with it. I can smell it. When I'm around people that are fearful I can immediately sense it, and my heart goes out to them. More than anything else, I think I covet the ability to minister effectively to people trapped in fear.

Fear is as old as history. Throughout history, people have dealt with it. You don't become aware of this so much in essays on fear as you do on stories of courage, boldness, and daring. We make heroes out of people who somehow overcame fear and were able to triumph over it. I don't think it's by accident that so many of our heroes through the years have been people who exhibited great courage. It's not by accident that Lil' Abner, that red-blooded American boy, would feel the way he does about Fearless Fosdick. Yet as I watch Fearless Fosdick, it occurs to me that he may not have sense enough to be anything but fearless. If he just understood the situation better, he would not be fearless.

Hollywood has been a little more honest with us. They've added the note of realism. There's always the picture of the youngster—quavering, afraid, pinned down by the enemy in some unseen position—looking over at the reassuring hulk of John Wayne and saying, "Aren't you afraid?" And John Wayne, in whatever costume, always replies, "Pilgrim, we're all afraid." And he's right. We're all afraid. We're afraid in different situations and for different reasons, but we're all afraid.

Franklin Delano Roosevelt came on the radio during his presidency and said, "The only thing we have to fear is fear itself."

One reason we've always had to deal with fear is that it's rooted in our beginning. According to Scripture, fear is the result of sin and death. Sin came and estranged us from the Father, and death followed. Fear was the harvest. Our estrangement from God leaves us fearful, uncertain of our situation. You can experience this in human relationships. I've seen it in large organizations where an employee would get crosswise with his supervisor and become fearful of the result. I've seen it in family structures where the child disobeys the parent and becomes fearful of what will happen. I've seen it in a thousand situations, but the author of each of them is our rebellion against God. Of course, the result of our rebellion is death, and the fear of death is the ultimate fear. So fear comes into our life and keeps us from living life fully. It makes us restrictive and protective. It dominates all other feelings.

In Matthew 25:25 there is a phrase coming in the parable of the talents that I have seen in a new light. I've always read it in terms of the unusual circumstances in which the one-talent man, rather than the five-talent man, would turn out to be the villain. Most of us excuse ourselves from major responsibility by claiming to be one-talent people. But in this case the Lord nailed that one-talent person and said in effect, "You are the villain." But that one-talent person was very, very honest. He said, in talking about what he had done, "I was afraid, and went and hid the talent in the earth."

How many of us have covered up who we are and what we could be because we're afraid? I know children who will not fully exercise their capabilities in a classroom for fear they might suddenly be in the spotlight and have to deal with the taunts of their peers. I know people in business organizations who hide their understanding of a situation for the same reason. I wonder if we do that before God. I wonder if we hide that which we know he's given us to serve him because we fear that we will not be able to exercise it properly?

Fear is the master thief that robs us of joy, of energy, and even of judgment. A few years ago, my daughter, Melissa, and I had been out West in a single-engine airplane. I came back and stopped off at a meeting in Nashville, put her on a commercial flight, and brought the plane back to Richmond, Virginia, a couple of days later. Somewhere over Kentucky on an instrument flight in a rainy, miserable-looking, summer low condition, the weather became turbulent. The rain was very heavy, and I began to be a little fearful of my ability to cross the mountains safely. I called air traffic control and asked them if the way was clear. They said, "We're not painting anything severe." They were talking about their radar scope, referring to what they see as painting. For me, they always seem to paint a better picture than it turns out to be.

I said, "Well, I don't know what it looks like on your scope, but I can tell you what it looks like out my window. It looks terrible!" He said, "Suit yourself. What would you like to do?" I said, "I'd like to land. What's the closest airport?" He replied, "Hazard, Kentucky." I said, "I want to land there." He said, "You want to land in Hazard, Kentucky?" And I said, "Yes, I want down!" He said, "All right," and gave me clearance for it.

I soon broke out of the clouds, but I realized that there was a wall of weather moving toward me. Then I looked down, and I realized why he was so incredulous. Hazard, Kentucky's, airport may be situated in one of the most picturesque spots in the world, and I'm sure if I ever have a chance to look at it from that point of view, I'll appreciate it. But from the air, trying to get down between those mountains onto that little strip, was another picture. I made one pass and missed it altogether. The second time I cut the throttle and came down in a condition I didn't want to repeat. I landed and thought I would burn out my brakes trying to keep from going off the other end. Later, as I sat thinking about it and waiting for the weather to improve, I decided that I had done a very dumb thing. I had taken the most dangerous course open to me. But I was afraid. I had lost my stomach for the whole situation. I can remember the terror to this day. I can remember the way it tasted. I had no judgment. Fear can rob us of our judgment. And fear can rob us of all the things that make life dear.

The Bible speaks of fear in two ways, and because of this, we sometimes get mixed signals. On one hand, it warns us to fear. In Psalm 111 and similar passages, it says that the fear of God is the beginning of wisdom, and that we must fear him. But on the other hand, Scripture encourages us not to fear. In Joshua 1:9 we read: "Be strong and of good courage; be not frightened, neither be dismayed." Many passages tell us not to be afraid and that there are resources to overcome fear. What is the difference? The difference is the source. That's a good principle for examining any motion. Where's it coming from? What's causing it? In any case, there are two kinds of fear.

There is a fear that is God-given. Let's call it a holy fear. It's the awe and reverence that he inspires in us. When people start talking about God as a "living doll," or use other such expressions, I worry a bit. I wonder if they have encountered the God that Isaiah encountered, for instance, whom he saw high and lifted up. His majesty so overwhelmed Isaiah that he was undone with his own sin. God does call us to reverence him and to fear him. Perhaps fear planted in our hearts that turns us to God, that reminds us of our restrictions, that points out that we don't ultimately have the answers to everything, is the instruction of the Spirit.

But the Scripture speaks at length about a fear that doesn't come from God. It's a worldly kind of fear that seems to be born of Satan and of darkness, that has the ability to crush our very lives. This is manifested in two ways: a fear of death and a fear of life.

Let's take a look at the fear of death. The fear of death is the father of fear. That's the ultimate threat, whether you see it simply as the threat of no longer existing, no longer thinking, no longer being able to retain all those memories that make you up. The fear of death is the father of fear.

But many of us also fear life. It is far more consuming. It focuses on things such as pain—pain that can grind us and break us down to the point where the fear of death becomes the lesser fear. This is the goal of terrorists and torturers. It's the reason that these people, under whatever guise or justification they might hide, are agents of Satan and of darkness. Purveyors of fear of any kind are people who get their inspiration from the dark side of life. It causes me to want to renounce any effort at any time to be the source of this kind of fear to anyone. Standing in the pulpit, I find again and again that the Spirit of God can use his Word to bring a kind of holy fear, but I pray to God that I will never be the agent of the other kind of fear.

There is a fear of the demonic and its darkness. People who have touched the occult and who have found themselves moving around on the shadowy edge of our understanding of life, sometimes come away marked by fear and by a sense of having encountered something altogether too foreboding.

Another kind of fear comes from rejection by those who should wish us well. There is also the fear that comes from enmity of those who would do us harm.

But whatever kind of fear, whether the fear of death or the fear of life, Christ is the only one who can help us cope with it. What instruction does the Spirit give to help us overcome the fear of death and the fear of life?

First of all, the fear of death has been overcome by Jesus Christ. No one else has been able to deal with it. The reincarnationists have made a run at it, but many of them have tried to hide under the rubric of the Christian revelation. The fear of death has been dealt with only through Jesus Christ. By his death he has taken on death for us, and by his resurrection, granting us the only hope known to life. If you don't accept that, there is no hope. Hebrews 2:14 says "that through death he might destroy him who has the power of death." John 3:16, of course, says in him we should not perish, but have everlasting life.

Jesus also deals with the fears in life. The Scriptures are very specific in saying that you deal with the fear of life through his indwelling presence. That's the thrust of the eighth chapter of Romans. In his indwelling presence, we have not received the spirit of slavery again to fear, but the spirit of adoption. In our sonship, Christ comes to live within us, to take up residence within us. Joshua 1:9 says, "Be strong and of good courage . . . ." It adds, "For the Lord your God is with you wherever you go." In Psalm 23, which believers have so often used to comfort themselves, we read, "Even though I walk through the valley of the shadow of death, I fear no evil; for thou art with me" (v. 4). Fear must be dealt with in terms of the indwelling presence of God. Paul understood this very clearly when he wrote to Timothy "Rekindle the gift of God that is within you" (2 Tim. 1:6-7). Paul was talking about the presence of the Holy Spirit. "Reaffirm the fact that God is dwelling in you," he was saying. Then he said, "For God did not give us a spirit of timidity but a spirit of power and love and self-control." God has given us a way to deal with fear. It emerges from the presence of God which the Scripture calls the Spirit of God or the Holy Spirit indwelling us.

According to Scripture, this power is the power to become, the power to stand, the power to cope, the power to endure things without losing faith. We are not helpless and hopeless. Peter says we even have the power to resist Satan. Instead of running and cowering from that which looks like darkness or evil, from the forces of hate or anger or violence or terrorism, the people of God are instructed by the Spirit to stand and resist in faith.

The second point is that the indwelling Spirit helps us deal with fear through love—the love of God. You say, "I though love was the opposite of hate." No, the Scripture teaches that it is the opposite of fear. In 1 John 4:18 we read, "There is no fear in love, but perfect love casts out fear." One of the definitions of fear is a heightened self-awareness. There is a point at which you are so conscious of yourself that any threat is just overwhelming. Love is self-denial, self-surrender, an outgoingness from self to others, to God, to the world. This is the reason love has the power to drive fear from your life.

The third way that the indwelling Spirit teaches the disciple to deal with fear is through a sound mind. You've faced hazards before, and you will again. You will come to a point where fear, whether in terms of illness or aging or sudden circumstance, will so come upon you that only the indwelling presence of God will give you the sense of order in your mind to walk by faith and to walk with your shoulders back and your head up. Only Christ can help us cope with fear.

I believe there is a fear of death with which a Christian still has to deal. I've looked at it with many people. I've asked myself, "What is it that we're really afraid of?" I think there are three things.

First, there is the loss of life itself. We love life. We find it more precious because of Jesus Christ, and we don't want to lose it. When I was with the Foreign Mission Board, I was living well in Richmond, Virginia. I liked my life there. I liked traveling about the world and being tied into a worldwide enterprise. I worked with some of the finest people in the world—those missionaries with whom I was so vitally related. I liked the experiences that were mine and the opportunity to write. Yet when God asked me to move to Knoxville, Tennessee, I said, "I've got to do it." There was some fear and trepidation. But soon I found a sense of fulfillment and happiness that I never dreamed possible. It happened again when I moved to Hardin-Simmons University. I think heaven and eternity will be like that. I think that even though we love this life, the minute we walk into the presence of God and Christ takes our hands and leads us into the new potential of what God has meant for us from the day we were born, we'll not look back.

Secondly, we fear pain, and many of us have dealt with pain. We can endure what will cease. If it doesn't cease by God's healing power, it will cease when he calls us home. Not too long ago, a friend of mine died of cancer. The minister said, "She's well now. She doesn't hurt anymore." Pain will cease. You can endure anything you can see the end of. And on the other side of it, you may find that God used it as the refiner's fire to do the last perfecting of our life for the new one that he has for us.

Finally, I think the fear of death that grips many most poignantly is, "Who will care for my loved ones? Who will watch over them?" If you feel responsible it is an especially troubling kind of thing. I remember when my wife and I went on a vacation when our children were small. We took them to San Antonio and left them with my mother and father.

But I remember the sense of peace that came as we looked back and waved at them. I realized that my mother and father were caring for them. I didn't have to worry. They could do it as well or better than I could. It has helped me realize that when the Father calls one of us home, he can care for our loved ones. It may look awfully dark from that point of view, but if you belong to him, he will care for your own.

So, the Spirit instructs us to submit our fears to God. Let his indwelling presence bring peace by filling you with his love. Many a person called to some great task has confessed that fear blocked the way. But they have subsequently been able to confess that a loving God gave them the victory over their fears when they submitted those fears to him.

Once more, the teaching of Scripture—from beginning to end—is summed up in 1 John 4:18: "There is no fear in love, but perfect love casts out fear." The spirit will so instruct in those places where we have to deal with fear.

15 Dealing with Loneliness

One of the most difficult problems a disciple might face in his or her pilgrimage is loneliness. As destructive as doubt and fear are, loneliness can be the most perennially destructive of all. Quiet and often invisible, it nevertheless has the ability to rob men or women of any age or clime of joy, of meaning, and of the will to live, and quite obviously, therefore, of their sense of being caught up in God's purposes for their lives.

Maybe you haven't experienced loneliness, but you've seen it in others. There are many testimonies to its poignant effect in literature, drama, and music. Country music has no peer when it comes to expressing loneliness. Maybe you've heard the sound in songs like "All By Myself," "Lonely Street," "Have you Ever Been Lonely?" or "I Ain't Got Nobody."

Think about loneliness not only in terms of overcoming it in your own life but in terms of lonely people whom you might encounter who need ministry.

Loneliness Is Everywhere

Loneliness has been part of man's predicament since the beginning of time. It is an essential ingredient in our estranged condition from our creator. Something is broken in our person that again and again results in a sense of isolation. John Donne tried to deny that: "No man is an island, entire of himself. Every man is a piece of the continent, a part of the main. Any man's death diminishes me."

That was Mr. Donne's argument. But I'm afraid that Matthew Arnold's words might be more where we live: "Yet, in the sea of life enisled, with echoing straights between us thrown, dotting the shoreless watery wild, we mortal millions live alone."

T. S. Eliot said, "Hell is oneself. Hell is alone." And Norman Cousins said, "All of man's history is an effort to shatter his loneliness."

I took off one day for a hike in the Smokies with a friend. We went up trails that were barely discernible to me, but trails he knew like the back of his hand. We had a delightful and beautiful day. At one point we climbed up a draw until we came to a cliff. Over it cascaded a beautiful, almost hidden waterfall. We climbed down to the base and felt the spray, despite the coolness of the day. But it was an unusual waterfall in that the water didn't run off. It just disappeared into the ground. I had a strange feeling watching all of that water come off the cliff and hit with such drama, and then simply disappear. We then climbed around the cliff and came to a grassy knoll where someone had once lived. Nature had all but wiped out the evidences. Only the various pieces of what had been the occupant's stove remained to show where the little cabin, with its foundation now covered with vines, once stood. I stepped off the dimensions of the foundation, and I remarked how small it was. There was barely enough room for me to have stretched out. Adjacent to it you could see where there had been a root cellar. It seemed someone must have lived there alone. I pondered the loneliness of someone in that kind of situation. I was sobered by a life that, like that waterfall, can roar across the precipice of time and then just disappear.

Everyone Is Susceptible

Loneliness can strike any of us. It can strike at any age. Some of the most devastating loneliness I've ever witnessed has been in children's lives. Some are isolated by circumstances, shut up in their own little worlds which they, after a time, must people with imaginary persons. Others are shut off from other children by the cruelty of playmates. They are isolated on the sidelines where they watch with little hearts breaking as the others interact and play together.

A vivid kind of loneliness can be seen in adolescence. Adolescence is often a time when a person begins to understand that he has a depth or a sensitivity that is difficult to express. They write poetry; they write music; they fill their days with dreams, and yet there is a sense of isolation. It's difficult to communicate with parents; it's difficult to share with anyone else feelings that are both romantic and fearful. And many adolescents become isolated in their loneliness.

I've seen young singles struggle with it as they watch their friends pair off and marry. The struggle to maintain relationships, to relate to couples in a meaningful way, to find the love and tenderness and care once accorded by family.

I've seen divorced men and women struggle with the void left. Even though their marriage might have seemed so destructive that they could not handle it any longer, the void afterwards is often a new kind of hell.

And when death separates people, and they no longer have the one with whom they had become as one and who had helped them relate to the world and with whom relationships had been made and maintained, there follows a biting loneliness.

But, perhaps, no loneliness is quite as devastating, as seemingly endless, as that which the aged feel. Some live in little rooms. That's all they have. If it were not for a radio or television, there would be almost no communication, because people they knew have died or they have lost contact with them. And they are isolated in their last days. How fortunate are persons who, in their closing years, find themselves in the midst of familiar surroundings, with loved ones who care for them, with the sound of voices of those they know, those who will speak a word to them every now and then. The alternative to that is the most profound kind of loneliness.

No matter what age we experience loneliness, it can be terribly destructive. We quickly find that it's not the absence of people that makes us lonely. It's a need for a real, meaningful relationship, an interaction that recognizes our value as a person and allows us to express ourselves. The Swedish movie actress, Liv Ulman, said in a TV interview, "Waking up alone is a kind of loneliness, but it's not nearly as cutting a loneliness as when you wake up with somebody and you feel alone." In other words, the real tragedy of our day is that, in the midst of people, we become lonely. We find ourselves cut off from those relationships that really minister to us.

Loneliness in the Bible

In 2 Timothy we read that Paul also experienced loneliness. Read 2 Timothy 4:9-12,16-18. Paul was lonely and was reaching out for some particular people: "Timothy, come to me. Get Mark. Bring Mark with you. They left me. I've been here by myself." He felt his sense of loneliness keenly, and he reached out for someone who would know him, someone who would identify with him and with his mission.

Jesus knew loneliness, too. Did you realize that? Oh, I'm not just talking about on the cross in the ultimate moment when he said, "My God, my God, why hast thou forsaken me?" (Matt. 27:46, RSV). I'm talking about that very poignant moment in Gethsemane when he had drawn aside to wrestle with his own soul over what God had sent him to do. He reached out and asked two or three of his disciples, "Come aside with me." He didn't want to leave them. He drew off just a little way to pray and came back and found them asleep. He said, "Could ye not watch with me one hour?" (Matt. 26:40, KJV). Have you ever been in the same predicament? Have you ever desperately needed somebody to understand you in a special moment, to understand what you were wrestling with in a particular situation? The Scripture says Jesus "was in all points tempted like as we are" (Heb. 4:15, KJV). He understands our human predicament completely. He understands loneliness.

Loneliness and Aloneness

Now, loneliness is different from being alone. Sometimes we need to be alone. Jesus demonstrated that again and again. A friend of mine, a college professor, once shared with someone the most meaningful time of his day. He gets up before the rest of the family, turns up the heat, puts on the coffee, builds a little fire in his den, and sits there with his Bible and has a time of study and prayer. It's his quiet place, and he says it is the heart of his day. He is alone, but he is not lonely.

Some of our college students talk about their quiet time and what it means to them.

There are periods when we need to draw aside. Many a young mother has prayed for a little aloneness.

Loneliness is where we need people who recognize us, people who have names, people who know our names, and people who can reach us and unlock us from ourselves.

Loneliness is sometimes circumstantial. That is, it is often precipitated by circumstances. We can understand the loneliness that comes from death, separation, or temporary circumstances.

Dietrich Bonhoeffer talked about loneliness in terms of prison, of even being isolated from other prisoners. But he was especially aware of not having the joy of relating to other Christians. He urged Christians to realize what an incomparable blessing of God it is to have access to other Christians with whom we can have fellowship.

Loneliness and Relational Skills

But more often the loneliness remains because we are not able to replace the friends we lost because of circumstances. We're unable to make and sustain new and meaningful relationships. We find ourselves locked into ourselves.

I'm thinking of two people. One was a college student, a young man who talked to me about the sense of loneliness of coming from another town. He had lived there all his life and knew all the kids in his school, and he had taken the friends and the few honors and recognitions that had come his way for granted. Then he went to a big college, and he found himself unable to replace those friends. He was unable to secure any kind of recognition. He found himself sitting in large classes, moving up and down a strip crowded with people, sitting in sporting events with tremendous crowds, and yet feeling all alone. He was unable to get out of himself.

I'm thinking also of a woman who lost the one with whom she had lived for so long. That could fit so many, couldn't it? She told me about the void. She said, "I depended on him to sustain friends. All of our friends related to us as a pair, and when he was gone I didn't have the ability. I did not know how. I no longer had the courage to get out of myself and go places and do things." She knew the kind of loneliness that strikes when we don't have the skills to relate.

Loneliness and Self-Esteem

The problem the psychologists tell us and the Scriptures confirm, is often one of selfhood. Can we call it self-esteem? More often than not, our self-esteem is too low. What happens when our self-esteem is too low, when we don't think of ourselves as highly as we ought? One of two things. Either we assume nobody would want anything to do with us anyway and that we have nothing to offer anyone and we retreat into the poverty of our own person, or we compensate by trying to exaggerate who we think we are in such ways that it comes out bizarre and repelling to people. So much of the boisterous, braggadocian, bizarre activity we see comes out of this.

In some cases the problem is not low self-esteem, but, rather, that of thinking too highly of self. The Scripture says we ought not to think more highly of ourselves than is warranted. When we do, there is a very good way to find out. When we think too highly of ourselves, we look down at other people. We look down at other people and think they are not worthy of our time or our efforts. Anytime you find yourself looking down at people, you're thinking more highly of yourself than you should.

The kind of self-esteem that Christ wants us to have should emerge from the Christian experience. It is a self-esteem in which we look at people eyeball-to-eyeball, peer-to-peer. I recognize your worth, and I recognize mine. How much am I worth? God, himself, thought I was worth his Son. God sent his Son to Calvary and the agonies of the cross to redeem me. I am of infinite worth. God wants me to confess that. I have gifts in my spirit. I have value to other people. But for the same reasons, I must recognize their value and realize we are both God's workmanship. In our loneliness we may be facing the instruction of the Spirit in self-esteem.

Loneliness and the Body of Christ

In 1 Corinthians 12 Paul talks about the "Body of Christ." The believing community is referred to as "a body." Each member is like an arm or a leg, which is a member of the body. It cannot function if you cut it off and put it someplace else. Some rather unsightly things would begin to happen. It would be of no value to anyone. But on the body it functions and has relationship. Paul says the eye is not supposed to say to the hand, "I don't believe I need you. You can't see." Well, it's not supposed to see. But the eye has an awfully hard time grabbing things, even a soft contact lens. In the same way, each person has his own particular worth. Such a relationship is indeed the "vital connection" as mentioned in chapter 4.

One of our mistakes is that we tend to judge ourselves by the wrong criteria. I've seen young men who, because they weren't coordinated and skilled in sports, thought they were of no value. They were using the wrong criteria. And I've seen young athletes who had all of those skills, plus the grace of a gazelle, but because they didn't have musical talents or relational sensitivities, thought they were a big zero, simply a "jock." They are judging themselves by the wrong criteria. Each one of us has not only the worth of God as revealed in Jesus Christ but also the worth of his or her unique personhood.

And in the church we are supposed to discover this. We can't say to any person in the church, no matter how different or how obscure his talent might be, "We don't need you." You can't say that. In extending the invitation to the church, over and over again I say, "We need you." Then I say, "And you need us." It's only as we recognize who you are as related to who I am, and who these others are, that we begin to function like a body. We need each other, and our loneliness begins to disappear as we recognize that need under the gentle instruction of the Spirit.

Loneliness as a Gift

In this sense, loneliness can sometimes in itself be a gift from God. Sometimes it prepares us for understanding and ministering to others. There are no words in the whole English language like "I know how you feel," when spoken in such a way that the person can believe you. All of a sudden they are dealing with somebody who understands. Maybe your loneliness will someday equip you to deal with somebody else, especially if you can rise above it in Christ.

Or perhaps your loneliness is a gift of God, the instruction of the Spirit, to remind you of a fundamental vacuum in your life. Augustine expressed it with incomparable beauty when he prayed, "Thou made us for Thyself, and our heart is restless until it reposes in Thee." Maybe your loneliness is a deep hungering for the One who made you and for whom your heart longs, though you know it not.

God Deals with Loneliness

God is the ultimate answer for our loneliness. Paul knew this. He reached for Timothy. He reached for Mark, but he said something else: "When they had all forsaken me, and I stood there, God was with me." You can almost feel his joy in the discovery. If you have had that experience of being by yourself, of having to cope with an extremely difficult situation, and then discovered the presence of God there, nothing will ever overwhelm you again. You know the promise of his presence.

Shadrach, Meshach, and Abednego are characters in the book of Daniel in the Old Testament. They were cast into a fiery furnace by King Nebuchadnezzar. As the king looked on the scene, he saw four people and said, "One is like unto the Son of God." It's a very strange statement, and it is not expanded upon. Yet, for me there is a clear message. In the midst of their trial, God, himself, identified with them. He walked their trial with them.

In the Great Commission, Jesus says, "Lo, I am with you always" (Matt. 28:20). I heard two people joshing at the front door of the church one day after the service. They were going to fly someplace; I believe it was an overseas trip. The lady of the family said, "I'm not sure I want to. I'm a little afraid." And the man said, "I told her that Jesus promised to be with her always." And she said, "Yes, but he said, 'Low, I am with you always.'" Don't let fear rob you of the promise. He is with us.

The Fellowship of Belonging

More than anyone else, God recognizes our need for fellowship, for fellow pilgrims. After all, he made us. In coming together and discovering one another, we not only present the milieu in which we can grow and become what we are to become, but we can experience that sense of oneness, that sense of support, that sense of joy, that fellowship of belonging that we desperately need.

The church is coming back to its own, among other reasons, because the increased estrangement of a secular society is causing people to hunger and thirst, not only for God, for whom their heart is restless, but for others who know God. They are seeking a fellowship of faith. Students are coming back to the church. They are tired of being just faces, isolated and lonely. They want to discover each other again in a meaningful relationship, not on the basis of what they have achieved, not on the basis of their good looks, not on the basis of their abilities or their grades, not on the basis of their economic standing, but through faith in Christ.

You don't have to be lonely.

16 Dealing with Stress

Once I made a promise (half jokingly, I confess) to preach a sermon on stress if I lived through it. This was during a period when we had been through a deep emotional and spiritual pilgrimate that led to a new post. We had endured the trials of listing and showing our house and looking for and buying a new house. We were separated from our children. And right in the middle of it, Dorothy had surgery.

I felt very much like the man who, early in the 1900s, tried to solve the yellow fever problem. Though beset with the fever himself, he feverishly took notes so that science could be further down the road than it was before. I tried to understand my own reaction to stress.

Yet our trials are often insignificant when placed alongside those someone else is facing. In the course of my previous ministry I had met many people who had to bear up under and deal with stress of a magnitude beyond anything with which I ever had to cope. I had a telephone call during that period from a friend in another state. She began something like this. "I can't believe this year. It began with a bad Pap smear followed by surgery. Then my mother died, and at the funeral my husband told me he was leaving me. I have had sickness with both of my children, and this week X-rays came back indicting my younger daughter has a spot on her lung." I thought, Oh, Lord, how could I have thought that I was under stress when compared with my friend's trials.

The World's Wisdom

I was in Mississippi some years ago with a pastor friend who had a rather humorous poster hanging in his study. This is the age of posters in which we have learned to speak to one another by graphic pictures and terse little phrases. This one was a picture of a small kitten who had caught the claws of one paw in the bottom of a great big rope and was just barely hanging onto that rope. The caption at the bottom said, "Hang in there, baby." Sometimes it seems this is the world's word to those who are caught up in periods of deep stress and of continuing trial—just "hang in there, baby."

One of the great anecdotes of history is of a king's minister who scratched in the king's ring what he said was the wisdom of the ages. His words were, "This, too, shall pass."

I believe there is a better word. I believe there is more encouragement than this. I believe we have more help in such periods than the simple admonition to "hang in there" or the simple assurance that "this, too, shall pass." I believe the following passage spells out such encouragement and help.

> Wherefore let him that thinketh he standeth take heed lest he fall. There hath no temptation taken you but such as is common to man: but God is faithful, who will not suffer you to be tempted above that ye are able; but will with the temptation also make a way to escape, that ye may be able to bear it (1 Cor. 10:12-13, KJV).
>
> (The Greek word is the same for both "temptation to sin" and "trial.")

Temptation as Trial

This Scripture uses the term "temptation." Temptation here is trial. In fact, a person who is caught up in and subjected to real temptation to turn from what he or she believes can be undergoing the most severe form of trial or stress. But trial or stress, in itself, is a temptation—the temptation to collapse before it, the temptation to curse God in the midst of it, the temptation to just give up.

Hans Selye, a German doctor who has done a great deal of research on stress, says there are three components: the stressor, his mechanisms of defense, and his mechanisms of surrender. Selye says that it is a mystery as to why mechanisms of defense are brought to play on one hand and mechanisms of surrender take over on the other.

But Scripture does not see it as a mystery at all.

A Common Experience

First, we need to realize that stress is a common experience. All God's children have problems. It is common to man. I have often had an experience in the pulpit that confirms this truth. I have referred to individual situations, carefully protecting the person involved so that no confidences would be violated. Yet I have had people approach me and say, "How did you know about me?" The answer is, "There hath no temptation taken you but such as is common to man." There are others walking this way. There are others being so tried. There are others in similar circumstances, also caught up in your predicament.

It is common to man, and that ought to remind us that there is no room for smugness. There is no place in which we can say, "Thank goodness, I won't have that kind of problem." "Take heed lest ye fall," the Scripture says. It reminds us that no one is exempt from trials or stress. And, invariably, in the midst of stress, we experience the instruction of the Spirit.

Stress Breeds Empathy

Stress is a part of the human predicament. But we can console ourselves with something else. In the midst of stress, we are caught up in something that will affect our lives in a way that will allow us to minister to others.

Once I was called by a young couple whose infant twins had died within a few days after birth. Their own minister was gone, and they asked me to come and hold the funeral service. I went immediately, not just because they had called me and this is what God had called me to do, but because I knew how they felt. Dot and I had walked through such a moment. I remembered my feelings. I know precisely what the man was dealing with and what the young mother was feeling. I went to them and said, "I know how you feel." It had a healing dimension.

Affirming Faith

Stress is common to man, and out of it we have that which makes us one. But there is more than that. There is more to say than, "Oh, yes, I know how you feel. Yes, I've been there." There is the affirmation of faith that we are called to make in the midst of whatever our trial might be. The great example for this, of course, is the biblical character of Job, who in the midst of losing everything, in the midst of suffering tremendous personal tragedy, cried out, "Though he slay me, yet will I trust in him." (Job 13:15,KJV).

If you will make such an affirmation, you will discover the beginning of that which God has provided to sustain you. God is faithful. That is what this passage says. And if in the midst of your trial you can say, "I believe God is faithful," then the resources that he does provide become a part of your life. Decide to believe him. Decide to believe that he not only can sustain you in the midst of your trial, but that he can lead you through your trial. You may have to believe in spite of everything around you, every evidence you see, everything you know.

Allow me to come back to aviation again. I turn to it often for illustrations, but it seems a parable of life. Several years ago a friend and I took off from Raleigh-Durham in a light rain and fog. As we climbed up above the fog, we were still in light rain and layered clouds, and I immediately sensed a very unusual and disturbing phenomenon. The horizon, such as it was, was a strong black cloud bank lying at a 45° angle to the real horizon. Only I did not believe it. I seemed to be in a turn, and a diving one at that.

As I scanned the instruments on the panel, which exist for just such situations, I confirmed I was flying straight and level. But my senses said, "No, you are in a steep turn. Do something quick!" My head was sending those messages to my hand, and I was trying to short-circuit those messages somewhere between my hand and my hand by believing that instrument. Yet something said, "Quit believing that instrument. It must be broken. You know the law that says anything can go wrong with a mechanical piece, and obviously it has gone wrong. Don't believe it!" But I had been trained to believe it. In spite of everything within me saying, "No, it's wrong; turn quickly; do something," I continued to fly according to the instruments and made myself believe that artificial horizon was the real horizon.

Faith is your artificial horizon. When everything else tells you that you are lost, when everything else says there is no hope, when everything elses says give up, when everything else would trigger these mechanisms of surrender, believe God, because he is the source of those mechanisms of defense that will sustain you and allow you to survive the situation. He will sustain you in several ways.

Faith to Survive

First, he will provide the ability to survive the situation. I think one of the best one-liners on war I have ever heard is the statement of the man who, when asked, "What did you do in the war?" replied, "I survived." He was giving one of the great testimonies of men and war. Sometimes just being able to live through something is in itself a victory.

I have quoted Paul's statement of faith many times. "I can do all things through Christ which strengtheneth me" (Phil.4:13, KJV). I have claimed it when attempting difficult tasks. Yet I believe that promise is never claimed more appropriately than when in the midst of trials, because it affirms that our ability to stand is not our own but the Lord's. "I can do all things through Christ which strengtheneth me." He will provide the ability to survive.

There Is an End to the Trial

But the Scripture promises something else. He will limit the trial. He knows your limits. He knows the point at which you can stand it no longer. The Scripture says, he "will not suffer you to be tempted above that ye are able." I know many people who, on looking back on the wreckage of events, say, "Well, he thought he knew my limits, but he did not know me." Yet I have come to believe, out of my own experience, that I have at times triggered the mechanisms of surrender at the very point at which God was teaching me faith. I collapsed before I learned the lesson the Spirit was teaching me through the stress. He will not only provide for us the ability to survive—he will limit the temptation; he will limit the trial; he will allow us to come through it. Faith says that in the midst of a trial, you can believe God will enable you to survive it. That, in itself, can come as a word akin to a refreshing rain in the midst of a drought.

Deliverance in Stress

But he will do more. He will deliver you. The Scripture says he "will with the temptation also make a way to escape." The visual term of the Greek is a mountain pass. It looks as if you are shut off. It looks like a box canyon. The passage implies, "Look up. Lift up your eyes toward the hills." It indicates a horizon of hope. God is there, and God will help you find a way out. He will show you a pass. He will show you the way through.

Many pilots flying in rough weather buckle down for a rough ride. They tighten their seat belts. They reduce their air speed to the maneuvering speed recommended for such moments, and they "Hold on." They keep saying, "It won't last forever. I'll fly out on the other side of it in a minute. I can stand anything, and this old airplane can stand a lot of things, and I just need to hold on." But I need more than that. I radio Air Traffic Control and say, "How about giving me a vector out of this weather." They have a radar scope showing where I am and the weather activity about me. They can see the shortest way out of it, and I want to know it. God is the controller in the midst of the storms of life. He is not only sustaining, but if we will seek him, and if we will seek his leadership, he will direct us.

I heard a beautiful testimony the other day of a man lying on a sickbed. He asked God to heal him, but no healing came; no deliverance came; no word from God came. But he said, "I believe." All of a sudden, he visualized Christ on the cross saying, "My God, my God, why hast thou forsaken me?" He saw the ultimate estrangement of man that God, in Christ, undertook for us, and he said, "I realized that I was entering into the sufferings of Christ and that included the silence of God." He began to rejoice at the revelation. Victory came into his life. His deliverance was not in the form of healing—his deliverance was in the form of understanding. When you ask God for a vector, when you ask God for direction, you are going to have to accept the direction he gives. When you ask God to solve something for you, you are going to have to accept the kind of solution he provides. If we were to hear only the testimonies from our friends to the kinds of deliverance they have experienced in faith, it would be an incredible experience. In fact, it would tax our ability to believe it. Many of you, upon reflection, know what I am talking about. God has delivered you.

Beyond Stress

On the other side of such experiences, what? The man of faith may find himself marked; he may discover that there is a scar. He came through it, but he has something in his life or heart or soul that will always be with him because of it.

In the book of Genesis we read of Jacob as he came to the Jabbok ford. He was facing the threats of his brother. He was dealing with his own sin. He was dealing with the trauma of the years in which he had slaved and worked to build something out of his exile, and now it looked as if it was all going to come apart. In the night as he prayed, he wrestled with an angel. He told the angel, "I will not let thee go, except thou bless me" (32:26). And he was blessed. But the next morning he walked away from the Jabbok ford, limping. The limp was forever a reminder, both of the trial and the blessing.

In the midst of our trial, in the midst of our stress, if we, like Jacob, could grab the angel of the stressful period and say "Bless me. Oh, God, I want your blessing. I want to learn." We may limp away marked, but we will also be blessed. We will have been instructed by the Spirit.

During the surgery I mentioned at the beginning of this chapter, I was sitting on Dorothy's hospital bed. I opened the Bible that I had brought to that room and read Psalm 4. In the first verse it said, "Hear me when I call, O God of my righteousness: thou hast enlarged me when I was in distress; have mercy upon me, and hear my prayer" (KJV). I had my word. "Thou hast enlarged me when I was in distress." Somehow in the midst of all this, God was bringing us to a larger place. Somehow in the midst of all this, God was growing me up.

In the midst of the trial, I was being instructed. "Thou hast enlarged me when I was in distress." The Scripture could be interpreted, "Thou hast made me a larger person, giving me a broader mind, giving me more with which to cope with life." I realized that in the midst of our stress, God was very actively blessing us. I hope you will remember this passage when it comes your time to walk through that which is so common to man.

17 Dealing with Grief

My daughter brought home her high school annual one time. We sat down and looked at it together because "old Dad" was interested in working through to those places where her picture might be and in having her tell me who was who and what was what and what possibly could have been going on there. It was an interesting time for me, looking at the life that she experienced day by day. But one page stopped me. There were three pictures. It was a memorial page for three youngsters who had died during the year. And I thought to myself, There's more there than just those pictures. There's grief and grieving. And then I wondered, Suppose they had included the pictures of the parents who had died and the brothers and sisters. I wonder how many pages it would take.

Grief is an incredibly common experience. Few adults have not already struggled with grief, especially when you include loss of a husband or wife through divorce or desertion or the tearing away of the fabric of some promising relationship. Grief is excruciatingly real here, too. But grief is a common experience and it, too, can be a place for the instruction of the Spirit.

Once, while studying the life of Christ, I came to that passage on the ascension where the angel promised that Jesus would come back again. I turned to a similar promise in 1 Thessalonians 4. I realized that the promise that Jesus will come again—what some refer to as the *Parousia* or the rapture of believers—is directed toward grief.

Paul says, "That you may not grieve as others do which have no hope" (v. 13) Christians ought to grieve differently. It's not so much that we will not have grief, but we should not grieve as people without hope do. Then at the end, Paul adds, "Therefore comfort one another with these words." So he was not only dealing with the grief of individuals, but he was dealing with the way the community of faith was to handle grief.

Most of us shy away from grief. "Tell me how to get rich. Tell me how to be happy. Tell me how to change my personality. Better yet, tell me how my wife could change her personality or how my husband could change his personality. Barring that, let's talk about winning others or even stewardship. But grief?" No, we don't like it, but I've become convicted that to avoid dealing with grief as an inevitable dimension in discipleship would be to avoid the whole counsel of God and some of the most important instruction of the Spirit.

Grover Tyner, a missionary in the Philippines, once told of hearing evangelist Jack Taylor lecture his group on prayer, and he just wasn't interested. That wasn't where he was. Even though he was a seminary teacher preparing young Filipinos for the pastoral ministry, that just didn't turn him on. But that night he dreamed he was a parachute instructor, teaching people how to jump out of airplanes. They were flying along with the door open, and he was pushing his students out one after another. The plane was almost empty before he realized that he had not given them parachutes. Something was missing. He woke up and didn't need anybody to interpret the dream. He understood it. To teach men to go out and preach or to pastor without teaching them to pray was like shoving them out of a plane without a parachute.

To teach people to live their days relating and loving and caring in Christ's name without teaching them about the difference that Christ makes when we lose and when we grieve would be a gross omission. We all lose, and we all grieve.

Sometimes grief is not the result of a real event. Most grief, if you were somehow to gather it up and apportion it into percentages, could be related to the anticipation of loss rather than loss itself. We're afraid of losing. We think we're going to lose. And we develop tremendous anxiety because of impending loss. But the Scriptures say we should cast every care on him because he cares for us.

Many people are not just dealing with the possibility, nor with some kind of free-floating anxiety, nor with a dimension that might be. They're anticipating an inevitability. The people who study grief are unsure whether it helps or hurts to try to anticipate grief. But we all do.

The stock market is constantly witnessing either buying or selling on the basis of good news or bad news that hasn't come yet. Traders just anticipate it, and they try to discount it. I don't know whether you can successfully discount grief or not. But I know this—Christ is supposed to make a difference in our lives when we do have to grieve. On one hand, he urges us not to borrow grief from tomorrow. On the other hand, where it seems inevitable, he enables us to face it with the knowledge that we're not going to be alone, and that as long as there is life, there is hope. God's power surrounds us whether it's enabling or sustaining or healing. It makes a difference to be a Christian.

But what about when grief does come? We're no longer talking about anticipation. We're talking about reality. We're talking about the numbing, ever-present, wake-up-and-it's-still-there thing called grief. Some people say that it's almost impossible to chart the course of grief because no two people go through it the same way. Others claim you can see three distinct phases in all grief.

First, there's the phase of shock. It's the numbing inability to grasp the situation because it's so overwhelming. This is the psychic counterpart to what happens to us physically. Often, when we are hurt badly, we feel nothing for awhile. There's a kind of a physical, God-created anesthesia that takes over. That often happens to our emotions in grief. We're numb. We can't grasp the reality of the loss.

And for those of us trying to reach out to people who are grieving, here's where we begin making some of our major mistakes. We assume that in this stage you ought to cry or that you ought not to cry. But there's no patented way to do it. We assume that you ought to be sad or that you ought to be glad. There's no way you can predict what an individual will do. In the shock stage you have to act mechanically, and you have to depend on the people around you. If ever Christ should make a difference, he should make a difference in the griever in the sense that he or she has someone to turn to and depend on and the knowledge that out beyond the numbness there are those who care. And in the Christian community itself, the difference should be obvious in the ability of believers to care and get involved.

The second stage has been called the stage of suffering. It's the long, slow adjustment. This is where it really hurts. This is that which just seems to stretch on and on and on. And here's where I made one of the major mistakes of my ministry. I made it with my wife.

Dorothy lost her father some years ago. I think I was very sensitive in the early stages. I tried to understand her feelings. I tried to step in where it was appropriate for me to step in and make the decisions and business adjustments and all of the things that arise from such a loss. But after a time I was ready to press on. I said to her, "Honey, now that's enough. You don't need to grieve any longer. Let's start living again. That's the way your dad would have it."

But grief is not like that. You don't just command it to be over. It doesn't just reach a time limit and cease. In our culture anthropologists say that we allow one year for grief. That's the reason some people put such social stigma on remarriage prior to a year. They say you ought to grieve for a year. That's society. That's convention. That has nothing to do with reality because each grief has its own time schedule.

But there is a third stage, and it's recovery. This is what some people, in the midst of their grief, need to know. There is nothing that tells us this more strongly than our faith in Jesus Christ. There is an end to the long corridor called suffering.

I read an article recently quoting a poignant letter on the subject. It was from a young woman who had been divorced and who had one child, a girl that was the apple of her eye. She lost that child to leukemia. She wrote quite rationally of the pain—a pain she described as so deep and constant that it was physical. It was a pain that colored everything that she looked at and affected everything she tasted and would not go away. She talked about suicide. Finally, the letter stopped because she quit talking about suicide. She did it. The article containing the letter pointed out how tragic it was that there was no one there to help her realize that no matter how deep her hurt, there was another side to it. She would come out.

The recovery stage starts when you're able to open some of the doors you begin to encounter. You are able to grasp some of your opportunities. It's not a clear-cut line as suffering is not a clear-cut line. There may be a reversion to suffering. There may be a reversion to shock. But finally relief comes and stays. We find that Jesus Christ has been active in our lives, bringing about this healing and nurturing in us the hope.

Our faith reasserts itself to affirm that those we have lost in Jesus Christ we have not lost forever. We will see them again. Christ's glad coming is not only our reunion with him. It's our reunion with each other. The body shall be together again from every age and every time. And that's our hope. We do not grieve as others grieve. That's the reason death has lost its sting because it's lost its finality in Jesus Christ.

But it's not enough to understand grief strictly in terms of the process because when we're grieving it's almost impossible to understand what's happening to us. What we must grasp is that we are not alone, nor are we to be alone. "Therefore comfort one another with these words" was Paul's admonition to the community of faith. Surround the griever with love. With it comes an awareness of the presence of Jesus Christ.

We are to minister to each other. Yet most of us feel absolutely helpless when we are around people who are grieving. What shall we do? How can we minister? Let me suggest several things.

First of all, people need to talk, and they need to talk about their loved one. We try to get them to talk about everything else. Somehow we think that if they don't dwell on it, they'll be all right. What we're really saying is, "I don't want to dwell on it." What we're really doing is refusing to enter into their grief with them and to let them work it out. It may not come out rationally. It may not come out realistically. That doesn't matter. Just hear them. How little it costs to give a listening ear.

Let's be involved. I once talked to a grieving friend who said, "You know, everybody was so wonderful. Decisions were almost impossible for me, and Christian friends helped me. And they listened to me. But then after awhile, I looked around, and they were gone. More than ever I needed people to be involved with me, to help me get outside of myself. But they were gone."

And we need to reach out and touch. I have often observed a touching ministry in a funeral parlor where a family is receiving guests or friends. People who wouldn't do it otherwise will come and embrace someone. A friend helped me to understand what was involved. He said, "Again, you are dealing with shock, and more than anything else, you need warmth. The warmth of another person who cares is the best kind of warmth. But more than that, you need tenderness of other people who care because you've lost someone who cared." The Christian community can make a difference here with an honest kind of caring that helps the griever make his or her way through that long grief corridor.

We've been called upon to minister to each other. Sometimes the person in grief is also dealing with guilt—either real guilt or neurotic guilt. Either way, they are hurting. The relief from both may come in a sense of absolution, a sense of forgiveness. Fellow believers may have to minister this to them in the name of Jesus Christ. If our own sense of forgiveness and the grace of God is strong, we can do it.

We are not to grieve as others. James said, "Religion that is pure and undefiled before God and the Father is this: to visit orphans and widows in their affliction, and to keep oneself unstained from the world" (1:27). Nothing separates us more from the world than our ability as Christians to enter into each other's grief.

The worst thing that can happen in grief is to grieve in vain. When we get through grieving, we're not supposed to be who we were before. We're supposed to be someone else. The worst thing you can say is, "She's just like she used to be," or "He's just like he was before." Don't waste grief. If God hasn't done something very special in our lives in the midst of the hurt, if we haven't come through the fire with a difference, we've wasted it. We've missed the instruction of the Spirit. We're not supposed to be back to square 1. We're more. We're more sensitive. We're more understanding. We understand life better. We understand death better. We understand faith better. We're not the same. Grief should never be wasted. Those of us who deal with another who has grieved should find that we understand what it means to be a part of the body of Christ as we've never understood it before.

Some years ago friends of mine, Theo and Guy Smithson, lost their only daughter. Julia was killed in an automobile accident. She would have been twenty-three two days later. She had been married less than two years and had no children. They grieved. As we sat in her home the night before the funeral along with other relatives and friends, Theo brought me a little devotional book. She would read it each night with its devotional thought for each day of the year. She said, "Look what I opened up for tomorrow" (the day we were to hold the memorial service). I looked at it. When I looked back at her, I realized what it had meant to her. The Scriptures from which the devotional thought was taken read: "Sorrow endureth but for a night, but joy cometh in the morning." We're not supposed to grieve as others grieve.

18 Completeness

And I am sure that he who began a good work in you will bring it to completion at the day of Jesus Christ (Phil. 1:6).

God's purpose for us—to redeem us and to empower us that in everything that happens to us we might be conformed to his image—includes the reassurance that he which hath begun that work will surely complete it. Yet most of us feel terribly incomplete. That sense of incompleteness can be one of the most haunting and emotionally disturbing of all feelings.

I went through a "winter of discontent," to borrow a phrase, when I was thirty-five. Always a bit of an "overachiever," I was burning the candle at every end that I could light. After a time, I developed some disturbing physical symptoms and went to my doctor, who seemingly delighted in assuming that my symptoms indicated something drastic. Gradually you could see his enthusiasm wane as he decided that, in fact, there was nothing wrong with me. But in the process of his working through the medical book to decide there was nothing wrong with me other than that I was pushing too hard, I developed a sense of dread. I remember going to see another doctor, an orthopedist. He was bending me around, making sure that I turned in every direction I was supposed to. Finally he said, "Jesse, what do you like to do that you haven't done in a long time?" I said, "Well, I like to fly." He said, "Why don't you do that?" I said, "I can't do that with these muscle relaxants you've had me taking. It's illegal, first of all, and I think it would be suicidal." He said, "Give up that medicine and start flying."

I went out to the airport the next day. Really, I hadn't flown in several years. A part of my physical problem was that I couldn't turn my head very far. Have you ever had that problem? They call it a crick in the neck, but mine was more like a dam on the "crick." I climbed into an airplane with an instructor who, despite my license, wanted to make sure I could still fly. We took off. Of course, the thing I had been trained to do from the time I had first begun to fly as a teenager was to look back over my shoulder after I cleared the runway to see how I was tracking out. I wasn't even thinking about my neck. As I climbed up and over the trees, I turned all the way around and looked back at the runway. It was a miraculous thing. I thought, Eureka, I've found it! Everybody just needs to learn how to fly.

But the problem was deeper than that. Possibly I was going through a bit of a depression, but the more I think about it, the more I feel I was going through what I have come to call "the onslaught of mortality." I had been immortal in the sense that death was somebody else's problem for about thirty-five years. By the time the doctor finished with me, I was mortal. It was my problem.

The thing that bothered me most was not the thought that I might die. I felt a deep sense of security in the Lord Jesus Christ. I was convinced that I would be with him, that I died the death of sin with him on Calvary's cross, and that physical death was now a door into his presence. That part was secure. What bothered me was a devastating sense of incompleteness. I had children that weren't grown. While they had the finest mother in the world, I was convinced that they needed old Dad. The work that I had been doing had given me a deep sense of well-being, but not a sense of completeness. I had published a couple of books and had another one just about ready to come out, but even that didn't promise completeness. It was this sense of incompleteness that made my mortality a most threatening kind of thing.

Paul Tournier, in his book, *Learn to Grow Old* (p. 169), says, "Life is a task to be accomplished. But who can claim that he has accomplished his task, that he has finished his task? The task always remains unfinished."

Yet it is obvious that Jesus had a sense of completeness. When he died, he said, "I have accomplished that which you gave me to do. It is finished." During that difficult period, I would think, Oh, God, if I could go home to you, whenever it might be, with a sense of 'It is finished,' that would be the most blessed thought I could have as I left this earth and walked into your presence. Then as I read Paul's statement about fighting the good fight and having run the race well, it was obvious to me that he had a sense of completeness.

As I gradually emerged from under my sense of dread, I came to realize that a sense of completeness is our right in Jesus Christ any time. Day by day, in the face of our mortality, in the face of the things that rise up the way we thought they would and the things that fall down the way we hoped they never would, wouldn't it be wonderful if we could live with the same sense of completeness that Jesus had? You and I have a right to have a sense of completeness right now—a sense of being in process notwithstanding.

I'm convinced that the instruction of the Spirit includes a course to help us discover a sense of completeness. Most of us seek it in the wrong ways. It's not just the world that goes after it in the wrong way; Christians go after it in the wrong way, too. You may say, "We're not interested in acquiring things as the world seems so intent on doing." But most of us have a pretty good running inventory at any given time of how many things we have. I know missionaries who talk about their missionary career in light of how many times they have lost all their things. It's a reverse process, but it's the same result.

When I first started backpacking a few years ago, I bought a book by a man named Fletcher. I like the ring of his name. It was called *The Complete Walker*. In this book I thought he was going to give me all of the skills I needed, but the whole thing dealt with the things I needed. I had been going out and backpacking and spending the night and surviving and getting back, and I didn't know what danger I was in. So I began to buy these things. Now when I go out, I can hardly walk. I've got all these things on my back. But I'm a complete walker. Well, many of us do that in our lives.

My former boss, Baker James Cauthen, had a way of saying, "It doesn't really matter what things you take with you if you take them in your hand and not in your heart." I think that's still pretty good advice.

Some of us look for completeness by developing skills. "If I can just get to where I can handle this skill, then I will have it made. If I can get to where I can sing like one of these people or do this, that, or the other like somebody else, I will have arrived. If I can develop the skills I need then I can be complete." We tend to look at a finished person as one who has mastered his particular profession.

Of course, we've seen kids get in trouble seeking to be complete in the thrills they've experienced. They have gone down so many blind alleys. If you're past thirty, don't think you're beyond that. In fact, there is another kind of problem that besets some Christians who have walked with the Lord, by the grace of God, right out of a Christian home where they have grown up with him into the adult world. When they get to about thrity-five or forty or even later, they begin to grow uneasy because out there in that world that they've been preaching against, there are people experiencing things they haven't experienced. Satan begins to work on them. He says, "You've been putting all of that down, but how do you know?" You say, "The Word of God tells me." He says, "Aw, how do you really know? Think what a better testimony you'd have if you would get out there and wallow in it awhile and then come back and preach about it." There's no completeness there.

Some of us just want to complete our schedules. I call it the "tyranny of the calendar." Man shall not live by bread alone; he needs his calendar. That's my sin. People ask me if I can do something. Too often I fail to say, "I'll pray about it." Instead I say, "I'll have to look at my calendar." It's almost as if I've laid aside the will of God and turned it all over to a calendar.

Some of us seek completeness by accomplishments. Now that makes more sense. Jesus talked about accomplishing that which the Father had given him to do. But what if your works collapse? What if all you give yourself to seems to come to naught? The crisis that faced many Chinese missionaries when the Communists took over that country, and they saw everything that they had given themselves to for years come to naught, was devastating. Many of them subsequently thanked God for it because he showed them what their real purpose in life was and where their real sense of completeness could be found. It wasn't in what they had accomplished. As the writer of Ecclesiastes concluded when he had considered all that he had done: "It's all vanity."

Sometime ago I saw a little drama on television, one of the most moving little love stories I've ever seen—*Phoenix and Griffin.* They met each other, a couple of the world's casualties, and fell in love. It was one of those things that made you smile and feel good inside. The only trouble was that Phoenix had cancer. The latter part of the story was about her death and Griffin's rage at having finally found meaning in his life only to have life, or God, or Satan mock him by taking it away. Ultimately, either rage or resignation is the world's only answer to the hunger in every one of us for completeness. Wherein lies completeness? It lies in Jesus Christ. He not only promised to make us new, but he also promised to complete us. Salvation is not a simple transfer of destination from hell to heaven. It is an assumption into the rich purpose God has for each one of us. That's the reason I began this book with a discussion of God's plan for your life. You're caught up in the hands of one who not only knows who you are personally, but who is working lovingly and purposefully with you and will complete what he has begun. Christ, in his complete commitment to the will of God as the ultimate form of completeness, shows us the way. Our commitment to God's love in Christ is the key to completeness.

In Christ we have the ability to live every day completely and the ability at any moment to be complete. That's what I want. That's what I covet for you. You'll feel incomplete while you're getting oriented to a new work. You'll feel incomplete while you are laying the foundations of some great project you hope to accomplish. You'll feel incomplete in the process of seeing it grow. You'll be devastated if something happens to it. You'll be overwhelmed if you're not able to finish it. But such incompleteness is inherent in the flesh. In the Spirit, God makes it possible for you to feel complete today and tomorrow and next week and next month. That doesn't mean you're a finished product. But you have a right to that sense of completeness that goes with being committed to his purpose.

Jesus said, "Take up your cross daily and follow me." Dailiness is the source of completeness. Paul found this kind of daily completeness. When he said, "I have finished the race," I'm not sure he knew exactly where the finish line was, but he had a sense of completeness because he was sure God did. He said, "I have fought the good fight." It reflected his inner satisfaction at having placed his life in the center of God's will in such a way that he had an on-going sense of well-being.

We need to recover the concept of prime time. Prime time for many people is between seven and nine each night on television. Prime time for other people is between the ages of eighteen and thirty-five. I read of a divorce settlement one time in which the main issue turned on who got the season tickets to the basketball games. The second concern was how much of her prime time he had used.

As Christians, we need a different approach to prime time. Every moment is to be prime time in our lives. We've been delivered from the time binders the world uses—the past, the present, the future. We live in the kingdom of God. The kingdom of God is eternity. Prime time is now.

Earlier I referred to Baker James Cauthen. One of the beautiful stories in his biography is the story of when Cauthen, as pastor of a very large church in Fort Worth, professor of missions at Southwestern Baptist Theological Seminary, and obviously one of the most exciting personalities around, felt that God wanted him in China. It was 1939. War had broken out in China. Many people felt it was just a matter of time until the United States would be drawn in. Hitler was on the rampage in Europe, and many people felt it was just a matter of time until we would have to deal with him. It was the worst kind of time to go overseas. It was the worst kind of time to take his two children, ages one and two, and his wife into "war-torn China," as they used to call it. So people made a lot out of his going. In fact, another missionary appointed with him in 1939 told me the story of their appointment. When they were recognizing the eleven people who were set aside as missionaries at the big Baptist convention that year and they got to Cauthen, the executive secretary at that time backed off and looked at the convention proudly and said, "Boy, we caught a big fish this time, didn't we?" I don't know how Cauthen's ego handled that, but that's the way they tended to look at him.

A few weeks later he was ready to leave. He and his wife, Eloise went by to see friends, their car packed for the trip to the West Coast seaport from which they would depart. Boxes were tied on the top. The seat had been taken out of the back and a piece of plywood fitted and covered with a mattress so the kids could sleep en route. Cauthen had even rigged an ingenious bottle warming process, utilizing the engine. They were ready to go. They were saying good-bye to their friends, Bill and Genevive Howse. Cauthen said something to Bill Howse that not only gave him a sense of well-being about what Cauthen was doing, but Howse testified it gave him a sense of well-being in his own life. Cauthen said, "Bill, many people are making a lot out of what we're trying to do, but for us it's simply the will of God." He said, "It's such a good feeling that I can say that if our ship is bombed in Hong Kong harbor and we never set foot on Chinese soil, I will have a sense of completeness because I will have been doing the will of God for me."

That's what God wants each of us to have. The process of being conformed to the image of his Son is continuing. Most of us feel as if we have a long way to go. Yet the sense of completeness that he covets for each one of us can be ours if daily we "take up our cross" and follow Jesus Christ.

Completeness is the intent of the Father in our lives. But completeness shines forth only from the image of the Son. The instruction of the Spirit, in all things, urges us to claim a daily sense of completeness. It adds up to practical discipleship.

And that brings us full circle. Does God have a plan for your life? Does your existence have eternal significance? Does the path of your pilgrimage have purpose? The intent of the Father in reconciling you to himself in Christ indicates a yes to each question. He reconciles you into his Son—baptizes you into his body; he begins to work a true righteousness in you to complete the righteousness that he imputes to you in Christ; he binds you to a body of believers in an intricate spiritual supply system. His goal is first, last, and always to conform you to the image of his Son.

The image of the Son is not ephemeral and mysterious. It has dimension, substance, and reality in the life of Jesus Christ. He is our model as well as our Savior. He is what we can become. His humility, his courage, his compassion; yes, even his spirituality beckons us and guides us down life's highways. The principle, power, and purpose inherent in Christlikeness is made possible by his indwelling Spirit through the application of his example in daily cross-bearing.

But it is a process, an ongoing discipleship under the instruction of that Spirit. Whether confronted with difficulty or doubt or fear or loneliness or stress or grief, his grace is sufficient and his instruction is sure. And while the process goes on and our sense of apprenticeship seems ever deepening, there is a true sense of completeness—not in ourselves, but in him—that is ours at all times.

Practical discipleship embraces this process willingly, adventuresomely, joyously, and gratefully.